Development Cooperation in Practice

Development Cooperation in Practice:

The United Nations Volunteers in Nepal

JOEL REHNSTROM

United Nations University Press

TOKYO · NEW YORK · PARIS

United Nations University Press
The United Nations University, 53-70, Jingumae 5-chome,
Shibuya-ku, Tokyo, 150-8925, Japan
Tel: +81-3-3499-2811   Fax: +81-3-3406-7345
E-mail: sales@hq.unu.edu
http://www.unu.edu

United Nations University Office in North America
2 United Nations Plaza, Room DC2-1462-70, New York,
NY 10017, USA
Tel: +1-212-963-6387   Fax: +1-212-371-9454
E-mail: unuona@igc.apc.org

United Nations University Press is the publishing division of the United Nations University.

Printed in the United States of America

UNUP-1037
ISBN 92-808-1037-5

Library of Congress Cataloging-in-Publication Data
Rehnstrom, Joel, 1959–
Development cooperation in practice : the United Nations
Volunteers in Nepal / Joel Rehnstrom.
      p.   cm.
   Includes bibliographical references and index.
   ISBN 92-808-1037-5
   1. Economic assistance—Nepal. 2. Technical assistance—Nepal.
3. United Nations—Nepal. 4. United Nations Volunteers.
I. Title.
HC425.R445 2000
338.91'095496—dc21   99-050730

CONTENTS

TABLES

FIGURES

ACKNOWLEDGEMENTS

This study is based on a Ph.D. dissertation that I completed at the Fletcher School of Law and Diplomacy, Tufts University, Medford, MA, US, in April 1998. Throughout my research, J. Dirck Stryker, Lisa M. Lynch, and Hurst Hannum provided me with guidance and advice, for which I am grateful. I am also indebted to Durwood Marshall and Viking Brunell for their advice on the analysis of the data.

I remain grateful to a large number of people who gave me comments and feedback at different stages of my research. Keith Krause and Tom Weiss reviewed the original outline of my research and provided useful suggestions on the overall approach and methodology. Steven Kinloch, Matti Vainio, and Giles Whitcomb contributed to my understanding of the United Nations Volunteers (UNV) programme and the concept of volunteerism more generally. Andrew Blane, Rene-Henri Bodmer, Michael Brown, and, above all, my wife, Eugenia Lizano, provided me with valuable comments, support, and encouragement throughout my research.

I would like to express my gratitude to Chris Whitehouse, who worked with the UNV in Kathmandu, Nepal, at the time of the study, and Deepak Tamang and his colleagues in the non-governmental organization "Search" in Kathmandu, Nepal, who carried out the data collection for the study. I am particularly indebted to the 14 surveyors affiliated with Search, who conducted the interviews for the study, and all 348 respondents who participated in it.

I am also grateful to Mari Poikolainen and Marjaana Jauhola, who reviewed and compiled information from reports prepared by the UNV, and Misa Fukunaga and Nayana Wickramasinghe, who coded and entered the data from the surveys into a database. Marjaana Jauhola, in addition, together with Yangtzee Tamang at the office of the UNV programme in Kathmandu, assisted in the time-consuming task of identifying and locating respondents for the survey.

Finally, I would like to thank the UNV programme for providing me with office facilities and access to files and reports, and for funding the data collection of the study. I am especially indebted to Brenda McSweeney, Bernard Fery, Bill Jackson, Renu Chahil-Graf, and Jean-Claude Rogivue, all of whom took an interest in my study and encouraged me in my undertaking without attempting to influence the results of the study.

LIST OF ACRONYMS

ANOVA	analysis of variance
ECOSOC	Economic and Social Council
FAO	Food and Agricultural Organization
G-7	US, Japan, Germany, France, UK, Italy, Canada
GATT	General Agreement on Tariffs and Trade
GNP	Gross National Product
Habitat	United Nations Centre for Human Settlements
ICAO	International Civil Aviation Organization
IDA	International Development Association (of the World Bank)
ILO	International Labour Organization
IMF	International Monetary Fund
ITO	International Trade Organization
NGO	Non-Governmental Organization
OECD	Organization for Economic Cooperation and Development
OESP	Office of Evaluation and Strategic Planning
SPSS	Statistical Package for Social Sciences
UNCDF	United Nations Capital Development Fund
UNDCP	United Nations Drug Control Programme
UNDDSMS	United Nations Department of Development Support and Management Services
UNDP	United Nations Development Programme
UNDPKO	United Nations Department of Peacekeeping Operations
UNDTCD	United Nations Department of Technical Cooperation for Development
UNESCO	United Nations Educational, Scientific, and Cultural Organization
UNFPA	United Nations Population Fund
UNHCHR	United Nations High Commissioner for Human Rights
UNHCR	United Nations High Commissioner for Refugees
UNICEF	United Nations Children's Fund

UNIDO	United Nations Industrial Development Organization
UNOPS	United Nations Office for Project Services
UNV	United Nations Volunteers
WFP	World Food Programme
WHO	World Health Organization
WTO	World Trade Organization

1

Introduction

Background and purpose of the study

Since its establishment in 1945, one of the mandates of the UN has been to promote economic and social advancement. This is confirmed in the Charter of the UN, and for more than 50 years the funds, programmes, and specialized agencies of the UN have provided assistance to developing countries.[1] Even if great disparities continue to exist between rich and poor, a generally accepted view is that international development cooperation has achieved economic and social progress – measured, for example, through increased income per capita, life expectancy, and literacy, or declining mortality rates among children.[2]

The effectiveness of development cooperation has been the subject of much debate, and while some critics continue to argue that aid is wasteful, a more commonly held view is that development cooperation can be justified on grounds that are not merely humanitarian. While recent research is beginning to show more clearly under which conditions aid can be most effective, what remains less clear is the extent to which different bilateral or multilateral organizations have been able to contribute to social progress and improved standards of living.[3]

A number of audits, management reviews, and evaluations have been carried out with respect to different UN bodies, but none of these studies really seems to be able to determine conclusively whether the agencies, organs, funds, or programmes of the UN have an impact on economic development.[4] In part, this can be explained by the fact that for many years, the primary concern of studies and evaluations of the UN, the World Bank, and other programmes was on the design and implementation of projects, rather than their outcomes and long-term benefits.[5]

In recent years, however, organizations such as the United Nations Development Programme (UNDP) and the World Bank have increased their focus on the long-term impact and sustainability of their operations, and the effectiveness of the work of the UN has come under increased scrutiny. An example of this is a recent evaluation of the impact of the UN operational activities for development, which was carried out at the request of the General Assembly.[6]

While the UN impact evaluation suggests that the UN system as a whole has been able to strengthen national capacities in the six countries examined as part of the evaluation, it is difficult to determine from the evaluation the relative impact or contribution of the different UN funds, programmes, and agencies viewed separately. The evaluation does contain some examples of where individual organizations of the UN have done particularly well or poorly, but since the purpose of the evaluation was to evaluate the impact of the UN system as a whole, the performance of individual funds, programmes, or agencies was not examined in any greater detail.[7]

Therefore, despite even these most recent efforts, information available about the impact of the work of the UN remains rather scarce. Meanwhile, considerable attention has, once again, been given to the reform of the UN, and a number of measures have been implemented to improve the effectiveness and efficiency of the organization. It is, however, striking that even the efforts aimed at preparing the UN for the new millennium do not appear to be based on thorough reviews of the past performance or achievements of the organization. In part this can probably be explained by a perceived urgency to reform the organization, and a reluctance to initiate comprehensive reviews or studies of the work of the UN that would take a long time to complete. All the same, the lack of in-depth evaluations is a cause for concern.[8]

What this study tries to do is start filling the gap of in-depth assessments of the achievements and performance of the UN. Recognizing that the task of evaluating all of the activities of the UN in the economic and social fields is enormous, the study focuses on a small part of the organization – the UN Volunteers (UNV) programme. The UNV programme is used as a case study of the development cooperation activities of the UN, and the study tries to show that assessments of the achievements and performance of the UN in the economic and social fields are possible and worthwhile undertakings, notwithstanding methodological difficulties and the considerable amount of time and resources needed to assess even a very small programme of the UN.

Scope and limitations of the study

The specific aim of the study is to assess the impact of the UNV programme. The impact of the programme is determined based on an assessment of the achievement of the objectives of the programme. In addition, the study assesses the perceived value of the programme to its users and beneficiaries, and, more generally, discusses methodological issues related to an assessment of the impact of UN programmes, funds, and agencies.[9]

The impact of the UNV programme is assessed in terms of changes in human and social capital as well as changes with respect to the availability of jobs, the level of poverty, women's lives, and the environment. The perceived value of the programme is based on an assessment by the users and beneficiaries of the programme of (i) the relevance of the work of the Volunteers, (ii) the performance of the Volunteers, and (iii) the results achieved and their sustainability.

The evaluation covers the time period from 1987 to 1996 and focuses on one country, Nepal. Nepal was chosen based on the size and length of the UNV programme in the country, the availability of different categories of Volunteers and types of Volunteer assignments, and the fact that the country was both a major recipient as well as an important supplier of Volunteers. In addition, it was possible to identify and train a group of surveyors to carry out the data collection in Nepal at a reasonable cost.

The idea of using more than one country as a case study was seriously considered, but in the end it was rejected in order to place the evaluation in a particular economic, social, cultural, and political context, within which to analyse the considerable amount of data that could be obtained from one country alone. Information and data from other countries visited during the course of the research was used instead to assess the validity of the methodology and the results from Nepal.

The study included a review of existing reports and previous evaluations, but is primarily based on new data specifically collected for the study. The study draws on interviews with 300 respondents: supervisors, co-workers, and other beneficiaries of the work of the Volunteers in Nepal, and a reference group of respondents who had no contact with the Volunteers, but who in other respects were similar to the users and beneficiaries of the programme. In addition, information from approximately 50 Volunteers who had worked in Nepal during the period covered by the study was used to complement the findings of the interviews and the other data sources.

Approximately 90 evaluations and assessments of the UNV programme were reviewed as part of this study, including one attempt at a more comprehensive evaluation of the UNV programme, which was undertaken in 1987. Experiences of individual UN Volunteers documented in reports prepared by the Volunteers themselves were also reviewed as part of the study, as were those included in the book entitled *Volunteers against Conflict*.[10] While that book contained the personal accounts of nine Volunteers who worked with electoral assistance, human rights, peace building, and humanitarian relief, this evaluation presents an in-depth assessment of the work of 50 Volunteers in what has been the main field of work of the Volunteers since the establishment of the programme – development cooperation.

Overview

Chapter 2, which follows this introduction, presents the context of the research: the role of the UN in supporting economic development over the past 50 years and the establishment and evolution of the UNV programme. Chapter 3 presents the research questions and the areas of focus of the study, and also includes an overview of previous studies and evaluation literature consulted.

The development of the methodology and the conceptual framework of the study are presented in Chapter 4, which also briefly describes how the data for the evaluation was collected and analysed. Chapter 4 also discusses the validity, reliability, objectivity, and relevance of the study.

Chapter 5 summarizes the findings of the study in three sections: (i) human and social capital accumulation and other outcomes of the work of the Volunteers; (ii) the performance of the Volunteers and the relevance, results, and sustainability of their work; and (iii) other findings of the evaluation, including assessments of the role of the head office of the UNV programme and the perceived value of the programme to the Volunteers themselves.

Chapter 6, the final chapter, summarizes the main findings, presents the conclusions and recommendations of the study, and discusses lessons learned that could be applied in the evaluation of other programmes, funds, or agencies of the UN. While the starting point for this study is very different from that of the book *Volunteers against Conflict*, mentioned earlier, several of the issues raised in that book are also discussed in the concluding chapter of this study; these include the identification of the UN Volunteers as true volunteers and the role of the UNV programme within the UN system.[11]

Additional details regarding the impact of the UNV programme, and the statistical analyses on which the evaluation is based, are presented in Appendix A. Appendix B includes details regarding the perceived value of the programme and the other findings of the study. Appendix C lists reports of previous evaluations and reviews of the UNV programme, in chronological order.

Notes

1. Preamble, Article 1(3) of Chapter I "Purposes and Principles" and Articles 55–60 of Chapter IX "International Economic and Social Co-operation".
2. See: United Nations Development Programme. *Human Development Report*. New York: Oxford University Press, 1997, p. 24.
3. See: (a) Cassen, Robert and Associates. *Does Aid Work?: Report to an Intergovernmental Task Force*, 2nd edn. New York: Oxford University Press, 1994; (b) World Bank. *Assessing Aid: What Works, What Doesn't, and Why*. Washington, DC: Oxford University Press for the World Bank, 1998.
4. Roberts, Adam and Benedict Kingsbury. "The UN's Roles in International Society since 1945". In: Roberts, Adam and Benedict Kingsbury, eds. *United Nations, Divided World*, 2nd edn. New York: Oxford University Press, 1993, pp. 1–62. See also: United Nations Joint Inspection Unit. "Accountability, Management Improvement, and Oversight in the United Nations System", Report 95/2. Geneva: United Nations Joint Inspection Unit, 1995.
5. Valadez, Joseph and Michael Bamberger, eds. *Monitoring and Evaluating Social Programmes in Developing Countries*, EDI Development Studies. Washington, DC: The World Bank, 1994, p. 227.
6. General Assembly Resolutions 53/192 and 50/120. Both entitled "Triennial Policy Review of Operational Activities for Development of the United Nations System". 25 February 1999 and 16 February 1996.
7. Report by the Secretary-General to the General Assembly A/53/226. "Triennial Policy Review of Operational Activities for Development of the United Nations System". 12 August 1998, paragraphs 18–35.
8. Report by the Secretary-General to the General Assembly A/51/950. "Renewing the United Nations: A Programme for Reform". 16 July 1997.
9. The need to take stock of the UNV programme was raised by several delegates to the 1996 annual session of the Executive Board of the UNDP, which administers the UNV programme. See: Report of the Executive Board of the United Nations Development Programme Annual Session DP/1996/19. 23 May 1996, paragraphs 59–61.
10. United Nations Volunteers. *Volunteers against Conflict*. Tokyo: United Nations University Press, 1996.
11. Ibid., pp. 221–225.

2

Context

The role of the United Nations in supporting economic development

Legal and historical background

The commitment of the United Nations to economic development is inscribed in the Preamble of the Charter, which contains a pledge by the founding governments to "employ international machinery for the promotion of the economic and social advancement of all peoples." Article 1, which defines the principal purposes of the organization, includes "international co-operation in solving problems of an economic, social, cultural, or humanitarian character...," and envisages the United Nations as "a centre for harmonizing the actions of nations in the attainment of these common ends."

The economic and social agenda of the United Nations is specified in Article 55, which includes a pledge to promote "higher standards of living, full employment, conditions of economic and social progress and development," and "solutions to international economic, social, health, and related problems...," as well as "universal respect for, and observance of, human rights and fundamental freedoms for all...." The responsibility for the discharge of the functions of the UN in the economic and social fields is vested in the General Assembly and, under the authority of the Assembly, in the Economic and Social Council (ECOSOC). The composition, functions and powers, and procedures of ECOSOC are set forth in Articles 61–72 of the Charter.

The efforts of the United Nations to promote economic and social progress and development were envisaged to be undertaken in collaboration with the specialized agencies, which are autonomous and brought into relationship with the UN, and through special agreements (Article 57). The role foreseen for ECOSOC was that of coordinating the activities of the specialized agencies, through consultation with and recommendations to the agencies, and recommendations to the General Assembly and member states of the United Nations (Article 63). This represented a departure from the League of Nations practice, where technical organizations dealing with health and economic and financial cooperation were developed within the framework of the League and operated under the general direction and control of the principal organs of the League.[1]

Documents from the preparatory conference in San Francisco, where the Charter of the UN was drafted, show that employment, economic stability, reconstruction, and development were to be central to the mandate of ECOSOC. To achieve the economic and social objectives of the UN, the scope of the work of the organization was to include formulation and coordination of global policies with respect to international trade, finance, and employment.[2]

The responsibility for the implementation of global policies was to be borne by the specialized agencies, including the International Monetary Fund (IMF), the International Bank for Reconstruction and Development (World Bank), and an International Trade Organization (ITO). Since the very beginning, however, the major industrialized countries insisted that global macroeconomic policies be dealt with by the Bretton Woods institutions, and multilateral trade policies be negotiated within the framework of the General Agreement on Tariffs and Trade (GATT) and the World Trade Organization (WTO) after its establishment in 1994.[3]

The failure of the member states of the UN to implement the original intentions of the drafters of the Charter made it impossible for the UN to fulfil its mandated role in the economic and social fields, and left ECOSOC searching for a role for itself since the very beginning. Despite this, economic development – understood as comprising economic growth and social progress – has remained high on the agenda of the UN.[4]

One way in which the UN has tried to promote economic development has been through special conferences and meetings and by bringing issues to the attention of member states at the General Assembly. These have produced resolutions and declarations that have played an important role in the formulation of an overall framework for international development cooperation.[5] The resolutions and declarations or their supporting documents have identified problems and needs of developing countries and proposed policy measures to address the problems and the needs identified. In addition, commitments by industrialized countries, such as devoting 0.7 per cent of their Gross National Product (GNP) to development cooperation can repeatedly be found in General Assembly resolutions and declarations.[6]

Resolutions and declarations of the General Assembly are, however, not binding on member states in the same sense as treaties or conventions are on parties to them.[7] As a consequence, what has emerged is an increasing gap between, on the one hand, the ideals of (at least part of) the world community, expressed in resolutions and declarations of the General Assembly, and, on the other hand, the lack of economic growth and social progress in many parts of the world. What many critics, however, fail to recognize or choose to ignore is the enormity of the challenges faced and the limited resources provided to the UN.[8]

In order to improve the work of the UN in the economic and social fields, the General Assembly adopted several resolutions in the 1990s with a particular emphasis on improving the effectiveness of ECOSOC.[9] Economic development is also an important goal of the proposals for a comprehensive reform of the UN, which the Secretary-General presented to the General Assembly in July 1997. The reform measures include, among others, the establishment of an

Executive Committee for Development – one of four such commit-
tees created to guide and coordinate the work of the funds, programmes, and departments of the UN in its main thematic areas.[10]

A persisting problem has been the continued reluctance of major
industrialized countries to discuss all aspects of economic development within the existing UN framework, where developing countries
have a larger say than they do in the Bretton Woods institutions.
However, these issues have not been satisfactorily dealt with by the
international financial institutions either. Other alternatives to provide guidance and coherence to the economic and social activities of
the UN system, including the Bretton Woods institutions, have
therefore been explored, in parallel with efforts to restructure and
revitalize ECOSOC.[11]

As many, if not most, important decisions on economic issues are
taken within the G-7 framework, it has been proposed to enlarge the
group of seven (US, Japan, Germany, France, UK, Italy, and Canada)
to include representatives of developing countries as well, in addition
to Russia which regularly participates in meetings of the G-7. An
enlarged G-7 could become what has sometimes been called a World
Economic Council. Another modification on the same theme that has
been proposed is to let the UN Secretary-General represent the developing countries at G-7 meetings.[12] Both options seem possible,
but the G-7 would probably only agree to meet with representatives
from developing countries from time to time, in addition to, or as
part of, the regular summit meetings.[13]

Other proposals to strengthen the development and coordination
of global economic and social policies include creating an International Development Council or the establishment of an Economic
Security Council.[14] Despite differences in these proposals, they
contain the major elements of the original terms of reference for
ECOSOC, which were developed in San Francisco in 1945. This
probably also explains the less than enthusiastic reception given to
the proposals in many industrialized countries, despite vocal proponents for them.[15]

Global conferences

Throughout its history, international conferences have been a way for the UN to address economic and social issues. The late 1980s and early 1990s saw a renewed interest in using international conferences, targeting national decision makers at the highest level, as a means to deal with issues of global concern.[16]

The global conferences of the early 1990s typically included lengthy preparations and intensive negotiations and culminated in summit meetings, with heads of states and governments signing conventions or declarations and programmes or plans of action. The first in this series was the World Summit for Children in New York in 1990, followed by the UN Conference on Environment and Development, which was held in Rio de Janeiro in 1992, with 165 heads of state or government attending.

A stream of global conferences followed the Children's Summit and the Earth Summit, including the Vienna World Conference on Human Rights in 1993, the International Conference on Population and Development in Cairo in 1994, and the World Summit on Social Development in Copenhagen and the Fourth World Conference on Women in Beijing in 1995. By the Second UN Conference on Human Settlements, Habitat II, in Istanbul in 1996, a certain "conference fatigue" could already be perceived among representatives of member states, and only 16 heads of state or government attended the conference.

What the summit meetings have shown is that the global conferences can raise the general awareness of important economic, social, or environmental issues among member states, and promote a common understanding of global issues. The summit meetings have also generated a certain degree of political commitment at the national level to individual and joint action to address economic, social, and environmental issues of common concern.

To ensure appropriate follow-up to the global conferences, mechanisms to monitor the implementation of conference recommendations and resolutions have been established. These include reporting on the development and implementation of national programmes or plans of action, and follow-up conferences five years after the summit meetings to review progress and achievements.

While the conferences have been able to provide some direction to the activities of the UN in the economic, social, and environmental fields, they have also provided the funds, programmes, and agencies of the UN with new agendas to implement. For many member states, the conference follow-up requires a considerable investment of time and resources, and has in some cases required the adjustment of already existing plans, locally developed solutions, and ongoing projects to globally determined economic, social, or environmental priorities.[17]

Operational activities

Even if the UN has not become the main forum for negotiating and coordinating global economic and social policies, it has from the very beginning supported economic development through so-called operational activities. This has been done through programmes and projects that have been, and continue to be, funded through voluntary contributions of member states, rather than the regular budget of the UN.

In 1949, the Expanded Programme for Technical Assistance was established as one of the first major development programmes of the UN. The programme was set up to enable the transfer of knowledge, skills, and technology from richer to poorer countries. This was done through the provision of fellowships and on-the-job training provided by long-term experts from industrialized countries.[18]

During the 1950s, other programmes were established, and the specialized agencies became gradually more involved in technical cooperation with developing countries.[19] Also in the 1950s, it became clear that technical cooperation could be much more effective if it was combined with low-interest loans or other forms of capital investment. A proposal to establish a special fund for this purpose was, however, rejected by the major industrialized countries, and when a United Nations Special Fund was established in 1958, after years of debating, it did not include a credit facility.[20]

In 1965, the Expanded Programme and the Special Fund were merged into a United Nations Development Programme (UNDP). However, the establishment of the UNDP did not produce the desired results in terms of improved effectiveness of UN development activities. In 1970, following a study on the capacity of the United Nations development system by Sir Robert Jackson, the General Assembly addressed the issue, and adopted a resolution that designated the UNDP as the main vehicle for UN development cooperation and the central coordinating body for all its development activities.[21]

Despite efforts to consolidate and coordinate UN-supported development cooperation, activities became more disjointed and fragmented in the 1970s and 1980s. The establishment of several new UN funds and trust funds for specific purposes contributed to this. Sudden cuts in funding on several occasions since the early 1970s also undermined the UNDP's central coordinating role, as did an increase in World Bank technical assistance, which made the World Bank the biggest provider of technical assistance to developing countries. Relationships between the UNDP, other funds and programmes of the UN, and the specialized agencies continued to be strained, which also made implementing an integrated and coherent UN approach to development cooperation difficult.[22]

In the 1990s, the development cooperation activities of the UN continued to be carried out through a complex web of funds, programmes, departments, agencies, and commissions. In 1994, for instance, 14 funds, programmes, or departments of the UN, 14 specialized agencies, and 5 regional commissions were involved in development cooperation. The total amount of support for development cooperation provided that year through the UN system in the form of grants was US$4.6 billion. This represents approximately 10 per cent of the US$50 billion provided in total for development cooperation that year.[23]

Each UN fund and programme reports to an Executive Board, and through the Board to ECOSOC and the General Assembly. To provide guidance to and coordination of the UN's development activities, what is known as "comprehensive triennial policy reviews" are undertaken. The recommendations of the past reviews call for greater coherence of the operational activities of the UN, more integrated programming by the funds and programmes, harmonization of programme cycles and procedures, and a more unified approach at the country level under the overall leadership of the UN Resident Coordinator.[24]

The establishment and evolution of the UN Volunteers programme

The idea of using volunteers in the development cooperation activities of the UN goes back to the late 1950s, and was first formally endorsed by ECOSOC in 1961.[25] Throughout the 1960s, the viability of establishing a volunteers programme for the United Nations was debated and explored. Finally, in 1970, the General Assembly established a United Nations Volunteers (UNV) programme, under the overall administration of the UNDP. The responsibility for oversight of the UNV programme lies with the Executive Board of the UNDP, which discusses the programme as an agenda item every two years.[26]

The UNV programme was primarily created to make qualified manpower available for development cooperation and to enable transfer of skills and knowledge that were considered lacking in recipient countries and were considered necessary for their economic development. In 1977, the mandate of the programme was broadened to include support to people's participation and community-based development activities as well. This reflected a thinking that was gaining support at the time that stressed the need to include people in the development process for external assistance to be effective. In the late 1980s and early 1990s four areas emerged as priorities of the UNDP, the parent organization of the UNV: promotion of jobs, reduction of poverty, advancement of women, and protection of the environment. Given that a large majority of the Volunteers at this time worked on UNDP projects, these four areas also became *de facto* priorities of the UNV programme.[27]

During the late 1960s, in discussions in ECOSOC that preceded the establishment of the UNV programme, it was maintained that an integrated and coordinated approach for utilizing Volunteers in development cooperation projects could further improve their effectiveness. This was the main argument for the establishment of a separate programme responsible for the recruitment and administration of the UN Volunteers. The establishment of the UNV programme also envisaged teams of Volunteers that, where possible, would be multinational and include international as well as national Volunteers. Volunteers from different countries working side by side has indeed been characteristic of the programme, and in the early 1990s the programme introduced nationals of a country working as UN Volunteers in their own country.[28]

Although no definition of a Volunteer was ever adopted, two were submitted by the Secretary-General as the basis for a discussion in ECOSOC. The first one defined a volunteer as "a person who gives his services without remuneration ... usually strongly motivated to donate his energies, his skills, his time for the accomplishment of tasks in whose purpose he believes ... a means of extending the work of an expert by demonstration and/or training, thereby helping to transfer a skill to local personnel." The second definition described volunteers as "men and women who give up their normal work and, without regard to financial benefit, devote their knowledge and abilities, within the framework of common efforts, to the people in regions of social and economic need."[29]

The role of youth as an effective force in economic and social progress throughout the world was seen as particularly important at the time of the establishment of the UNV programme. Since its establishment, however, the programme has tried to distance itself from a notion of Volunteers as young people, even if the General Assembly in the late 1960s was "convinced that the United Nations could respond imaginatively to the desire of individuals – and in particular youth, irrespective of country, class, race, religion, sex, age, economic level or social status – to dedicate a certain period of their lives to the cause of development, and could offer them a positive means of translating their concern for their fellow men into an effective force for economic and social progress throughout the world."[30]

What the programme, however, has tried to do is promote volunteerism more generally. To this effect the General Assembly approved two resolutions – one urging that 5 December each year be celebrated as International Volunteers Day, and a second one proclaiming the year 2001 as the International Year of Volunteers.[31]

Since its establishment, the UNV programme has been demand driven, and in its first 30 years the programme has evolved and grown considerably in terms of the number of Volunteers fielded, countries served, and nationalities participating in the programme. In 1971, the first 35 UN Volunteers were fielded in 5 countries. Throughout the 1970s, the number of Volunteers increased, and in 1981 a total of 1,330 Volunteers served in almost 90 countries.[32]

During the 1980s, particularly the late 1980s, and the 1990s, the programme continued growing, reaching, in 1993, a total of 3,590 Volunteers from 119 different countries serving in 125 countries. In the following years the total number of Volunteers decreased somewhat, but the number of countries served and nationalities serving increased. During 1996, a total of 3,242 Volunteers, from 125 countries, served with the programme in 136 different countries. By the end of that year a total of 14,524 Volunteers from more than 140 nations had worked in an equal number of countries. 1997 and 1998 saw further growth in the number of Volunteers, with a total of 3,620 and 4,047 Volunteers fielded, respectively, in each year.

The UNV programme has also expanded its areas of work considerably, particularly in the 1990s. In addition to assignments in the traditional areas of focus of the UNV programme – transfer of skills and knowledge and community development – UN Volunteers have worked in private sector development, humanitarian emergencies, peace building, human rights, and electoral assistance programmes.

In a direct response to the demand for UN Volunteers to work in complex emergencies, a separate humanitarian relief unit was established as part of the programme in 1991.

In the 1980s, 95 per cent of all Volunteers worked in development cooperation, in areas such as agriculture, forestry, fisheries, health, education, vocational training, planning, administration, and social mobilization. By 1993, the proportion of UN Volunteers working in development cooperation had fallen to 77 per cent. At the same time, 13 per cent worked with humanitarian relief and 10 per cent with peace building and electoral assistance. In 1996, 69 per cent of the Volunteers worked with development cooperation, 24 per cent with humanitarian relief and 7 per cent with peace building, human rights, or electoral assistance.

In the 1990s, the total annual expenditure of the UNV programme ranged from US$44 to US$64 million, which makes it a rather modest UN programme in terms of its size. During the first half of the 1990s, approximately US$40 million of the total expenditure of the programme per year was for development activities. In comparison, the total expenditure of the UN system on development activities, excluding those of the international financial institutions, was around US$4.5 billion per year in the early 1990s. The funding for development cooperation channeled through the UNV programme thus represented approximately 1 per cent of all UN development cooperation expenditure during this period.[33]

Throughout the first two decades of the UNV programme, almost all of the funding for the programme came from the UNDP; in 1989, for example, 85 per cent of the funding for the UNV programme was provided by the UNDP. In the early 1990s this began to change, reflecting the new areas that the programme embarked upon. In 1993, the contribution of the UNDP to the programme had fallen to 56 per cent, while other UN organizations and departments contributed almost 22 per cent of the programme's budget. Direct contributions by member states to trust funds of the programme accounted for another 22 per cent. By 1996, the contribution of the UNDP had declined further and stood at 20 per cent. Trust

funds accounted for 36 per cent, and UN organizations and departments contributed 44 per cent of the resources of the programme.

Traditionally, most UN Volunteers have worked on projects for
different UN organizations or departments and the specialized
agencies. Important hosts of Volunteers over the years – in addition
to government ministries and institutions – include the UN Office
for Project Services (UNOPS), which executes a large number of
UNDP-funded projects, the World Food Programme (WFP), the
UN Children's Fund (UNICEF), and the UN Population Fund
(UNFPA).

Other hosts of relatively large numbers of Volunteers in the 1980s
and 1990s include the UN Department of Economic and Social
Affairs, the UN Centre for Human Settlements (Habitat), and the
specialized agencies, such as the Food and Agricultural Organization
(FAO), the International Labour Organization (ILO), the World
Health Organization (WHO) and the UN Industrial Development
Organization (UNIDO), the UN Educational, Scientific, and Cul-
tural Organization (UNESCO), the International Civil Aviation
Organization (ICAO), and the International Development Associa-
tion of the World Bank (IDA).[34]

In the early and mid-1990s, the UN High Commissioner for
Refugees (UNHCR) and the UN High Commissioner for Human
Rights (UNHCHR) became two of the main users of Volunteers.
The single biggest user of UN Volunteers to date, however, has
been the United Nations Department of Peacekeeping Operations
(UNDPKO), with 483 and 466 Volunteers, respectively, working
under the umbrella of the UNDPKO in 1996 and 1997. The number of Volunteers serving with the different agencies in different
years is shown in Table 2.1 (pages 20 and 21).

Over the years, the largest numbers of Volunteers have worked in
Africa; in 1996 almost one-half of all Volunteers served in Africa. In
the same year, one-fifth of the Volunteers worked in Asia and the
Pacific, and almost the same number served in Latin America and the
Caribbean. The rest worked in the Middle East, Central and Eastern
Europe, the Baltic States, and the Commonwealth of Independent

States. Two-thirds of the Volunteers served in the 48 countries that are classified by the United Nations as least developed.

An important aspect of the UNV programme has been its universality, and the fact that it is one of very few programmes that provide opportunities for nationals of developing countries to work as Volunteers in other developing countries. In 1996, of the 3,242 Volunteers who served during the year, 2,285, or 70 per cent, came from 94 different developing countries. The other 957 Volunteers, or 30 per cent, came from 31 different industrialized countries.

During the first two decades of the programme, all UN Volunteers were internationally recruited, but since the early 1990s, when the first national Volunteers were fielded, more and more Volunteers have been recruited locally to work in their own countries. In 1996, 356 of the total 3,242 Volunteers were national Volunteers. The biggest number of national Volunteers, 139, worked in Latin America and the Caribbean, where they accounted for 25 per cent of all Volunteers. In the other regions, the national Volunteers accounted for between 3 and 20 per cent of all Volunteers.

The UNV programme has made a conscious effort to try to distance itself from a notion of Volunteers as people who are young and inexperienced – despite several resolutions of the General Assembly linking the UN Volunteers and youth programmes.[35] Instead, the UNV programme has emphasized experience, qualifications, and motivation in the selection of Volunteers. In 1996, almost 90 per cent of the Volunteers were over 30, and the average age was 39 years. Half of the Volunteers had more than 10 years of work experience, and some had more than 30 years. One-fourth of the Volunteers had between 6 and 10 years of work experience and the remaining fourth had 5 years or less.

Approximately one-third of the Volunteers had a post-graduate degree and another third held a first university degree. Around one-fifth had a diploma or certificate from a technical or vocational institute. The rest, many of whom worked in areas for which an academic degree or technical education may not necessarily be the best preparation, such as community development, had a general

Table 2.1 Total number of Volunteers serving globally with different UN organizations during the period covered by the study

	1987	1988	1989	1990	1991	1992	1993	1994	1995	1996
UN High Commissioner for Refugees	26	27	23	33	30	38	108	165	157	205
UN Office for Project Services	45	52	53	72	105	118	121	131	197	203
World Food Programme	49	41	44	48	68	76	106	121	125	109
UN High Commissioner for Human Rights									54	100
UN Children's Fund	31	25	36	36	54	66	97	92	101	92
UN Population Fund				8	15	8	17	36	59	72
International Labour Organization	111	121	140	128	110	98	136	108	92	70
UN Department for Economic and Social Affairs	70	98	112	118	96	63	80	127	130	68
World Health Organization	18	25	32	33	41	45	77	83	67	56
Food and Agriculture Organization	109	154	185	219	192	162	166	113	66	42
UN Development Programme		19	28	33	22	39	48	50	57	39
UN Centre for Human Settlements	20	19	19	23	23	27	28	31	36	36
UN Industrial Development Organization	23	21	40	42	32	28	36	22	13	19
International Civil Aviation Organization	23	22	17	13	11		7	14	17	15
UN Educational, Scientific, and Cultural Organization	34	36	37	31	33	21	43	37	25	14

	1987	1988	1989	1990	1991	1992	1993	1994	1995	1996
World Bank/IDA	11	10	4	5	12	13	34	32	29	14
International Trade Centre	6	6	7	9	6	4	5	2	3	4
UN Conference on Trade and Development	1	3			1		1	1	1	4
World Tourism Organisation		1	1						2	4
Asian Development Bank	3	2	2	3	2	4	3	2	2	3
UN Capital Development Fund							2		3	3
World Meteorological Organization	5	7	10	13	9	4	6	4	3	1
UN Economic and Social Commission for Asia and the Pacific	1	3	4	4	3	3	1	1	1	1
UN Economic Commission for Africa	3	4	2	5	4	1	2			
International Maritime Organisation		1								
UN Disaster Relief Organisation		1	1	7	4	1	1	1	1	
UN Department of Peace-keeping									310	483
Others		10	3	10	9	12	13	21	9	23
Unaccounted	23	18	20	9	4	3	12	2	2	0
Reported total in UN agency projects	612	726	819	902	887	834	1152	1196	1562	1680
Government executed projects	43	63	74	58	80	138	247	366	347	347
UNV executed projects	614	745	908	1095	1094	1517	2191	1940	1354	1215
Grand total	1269	1534	1801	2055	2061	2489	3590	3502	3263	3242

secondary level education. In 1996, the number of male Volunteers was twice that of female Volunteers.[36]

Two main categories of Volunteers exist: UNV specialists and UNV community workers. UNV specialists have typically worked with government ministries or departments and projects of international organizations. Occasionally, and perhaps increasingly, UNV specialists also work with non-governmental organizations and communities. This, however, is more characteristic of the UNV community workers.

Another characteristic of the UNV community worker assignments has been their concentration in a relatively few countries in Africa and Asia. In 1979, when the first 37 UNV community workers were fielded, they accounted for 5 per cent of the total number of UN Volunteers. In 1989, the UNV community workers represented 10 per cent of the total number of UN Volunteers. In 1993, the corresponding figure was 15 per cent, and in 1996, 7 per cent. In part this drop in the number of community worker assignments reflects an increased focus by the programme on national UN Volunteers – another low-cost UNV programme modality.

The Volunteers receive a monthly living allowance that in 1996, depending on the cost of living at the duty station, ranged from US$700 to US$1,100 for UNV specialists without a family. For married UNV specialists, the allowance varied between US$1,100 and US$1,700. For UNV community workers, the monthly living allowance ranged from US$150 to US$400, depending on the cost of living at the duty station. All UNV community workers at any given duty station receive the same allowance irrespective of their marital status.

In addition to the monthly living allowance, the Volunteers are paid a settling-in and repatriation grant as well as travel to and from their country of assignment. The Volunteers are covered by medical insurance, and are provided housing, furniture, and transportation to and from work, or an equivalent amount to cover these costs. In addition, the programme provides orientation and training of the Volunteers.

The total costs of a Volunteer assignment vary considerably between countries as well as within countries, depending on the cost of
living at each duty station. In 1996, the estimated average annual
cost of a UNV specialist was US$32,000. For a UNV community
worker, the corresponding figure was US$7,000. In addition, the
average administrative costs for each Volunteer amounted to
US$5,400 per year.[37]

Comparing the costs of UN Volunteer assignments to those of
volunteers from other programmes is difficult because of differences
in ways of recording expenditures. Rough comparisons can, however,
be made and figures available from 1994 indicate that the UNV
community workers, even with the administrative costs included, are
among the least costly international volunteers available for development cooperation. The same figures place UNV specialists at the
middle of a list that presents the costs of volunteers from 28 different
volunteer sending agencies.[38]

Compared to other expatriate staff recruited to work on programmes or projects of the UN, the UN Volunteers are considerably
less expensive. The average annual cost of these other expatriate staff,
often referred to as "experts", is in most cases well over US$100,000.
Although UN organizations still use highly paid expatriate staff for
certain assignments, in many instances UNV specialists are used to
carry out work that in the past was done by resident long-term
experts. While the professional qualifications and experience of the
UN Volunteers certainly have been important considerations for UN
organizations in deciding to use UN Volunteers, cost considerations
have also no doubt influenced the decision-making.

The cost of the Volunteers is one important way in which the
UNV programme has tried to market itself, and if the number of
Volunteer assignments is used as a criterion, the programme seems
quite successful. What the programme appears to have been less
successful in is dealing with a perception of the Volunteers as a
category distinct from, and not quite as good as, other UN staff,
and therefore sometimes viewed as "second-class workers" or "cheap
labour".[39]

Notes

1. For a more extensive discussion of differences between the UN and the League of Nations in the economic and social fields, see Goodrich, Leland M. "From League of Nations to United Nations". *International Organization* 1, pp. 3–21, 1947.

2. *Report of the Preparatory Commission of the United Nations*, PC/20. Chapter III, Section 4, 23 December 1945, paragraphs 18–25.

3. The World Bank and the International Monetary Fund are often referred to as "The Bretton Woods Institutions" after Bretton Woods, New Hampshire, US, where the two institutions were founded at a conference in July 1944. The refusal of the US to agree to the establishment of the International Trade Organization meant that the GATT, which was originally intended as an interim arrangement, became the main forum for multilateral trade negotiations. GATT ceased to exist and became the WTO on 1 January 1995, following an agreement reached in April 1994. For an overview of the political context of the economic and social activities of the UN, see Dadzie, Kenneth. "The UN and the Problem of Economic Development". In: Roberts, Adam and Benedict Kingsbury, eds. *United Nations, Divided World*, 2nd edn. New York: Oxford University Press, 1993, pp. 297–311.

4. While economic growth in this study is defined simply as an increase in GNP, economic development is used to imply social progress in addition to an increase in per capita income. This includes participation of people in the process of development through the production as well as enjoyment of the benefits of development. See Gillis, Malcolm, Dwight H. Perkins, Michael Roemer, and Donald R. Snodgrass. *Economics of Development*, 3rd edn. New York: W.W. Norton & Co., 1992, pp. 8–9.

5. See for instance the four declarations proclaiming UN development decades: (a) General Assembly Resolution No. 1710 (XVI). "United Nations Development Decade". 18 December 1961; (b) Resolution No. 2626 (XXIV). "International Development Strategy for the Second United Nations Development Decade". 24 October 1970; (c) Resolution No. 35/56. "International Development Strategy for the Third United Nations Development Decade". 5 December 1980; (d) Resolution No. 45/199. "International Development Strategy for the Fourth United Nations Development Decade". 21 December 1990. Other declarations often mentioned as important include: (a) Resolution 2542 (XXIV). "Declaration on Social Progress and Development". 11 December 1969; (b) Resolution No. 3201 (S-VI). "A New International Economic Order". 1 May 1974; (c) Resolution No. 41/128. "Declaration on the Right to Development". 4 December 1986; (d) Resolution No. S-18/3. "Declaration on International Economic Cooperation, in Particular the Revitalization of Economic Growth and Development of the Developing Countries". 1 May 1990; (e) Resolution No. 51/240. "Agenda for Development". 20 June 1997.

6. While most industrialized countries have accepted the target of contributing 0.7 per cent of GNP towards development cooperation, only four – Denmark,

Norway, Sweden, and the Netherlands – have actually reached and maintained this target. See: the Organization for Economic Cooperation and Development. *Development Cooperation Report, 1998*, Development Assistance Committee. Paris: OECD, 1999, p. 31.

7. For a discussion on the normative effects of General Assembly resolutions, see: (a) Kirgis, Frederic L. Jr. *International Organizations in their Legal Setting*, 2nd edn. St. Paul: West Publishing Co., 1993, pp. 333–351; (b) Kaufmann, Johann and Nico Schrijver. *Changing Global Needs: The Expanding Roles for the United Nations System*. Hanover, NH: The Academic Council on the United Nations System, 1990, pp. 29–36.

8. Kirgis, Frederic L. Jr. *International Organizations in their Legal Setting*, 2nd edn. St. Paul: West Publishing Co., 1993, p. 223. See also: Eberstadt, Nicholas. "The Impact of UN's 'Development Activities' on Third World Development". In: Ted Galen Carpentier, ed. *Delusions of Grandeur. The United Nations and Global Intervention*. Washington, DC: The Cato Institute, 1997, pp. 213–225.

9. General Assembly Resolutions 50/227 and 48/162. Both entitled "Further Measures for the Restructuring and Revitalization of the United Nations in the Economic, Social and Related Fields". 16 May 1996 and 14 January 1994; Resolutions 46/235, 45/264, and 45/177. All entitled "Restructuring and Revitalization of the United Nations in the Economic, Social and Related Fields". 13 April 1992, 13 May 1991, and 19 December 1990.

10. Report by the Secretary-General to the General Assembly A/51/950. "Renewing the United Nations: A Programme for Reform". 16 July 1997. For a review of earlier proposals for reform of the economic and social sectors of the UN, see Kaufmann, Johann and Nico Schrijver. *Changing Global Needs: The Expanding Roles for the United Nations System*. Hanover, NH: The Academic Council on the United Nations System, 1990, pp. 40–43.

11. See: Childers, Erskine with Brian Urquhart. *Renewing the United Nations System*. Uppsala: Dag Hammarskjold Foundation, 1994, pp. 53–86; or The Report of the Independent Working Group on the Future of the United Nations. *The United Nations in its Second Half-Century*. New Haven, CT: Yale University Printing Service, 1995, pp. 25–34.

12. World Institute for Development Economics Research of the United Nations University. *World Economic Summits: The Role of Representative Groups in the Governance of the World Economy*, Study Group Series No. 4. Helsinki: WIDER, 1989; and Jakobson, Max. *The United Nations in the 1990s. A Second Chance?* New York: Twentieth Century Books, 1993, pp. 150–154.

13. A first step in this direction may have been the 1996 Lyon summit of the G-7, where not only the UN Secretary-General participated, but also the executive heads of the International Monetary Fund, the World Bank and the World Trade Organization. Participation other than as an observer is, however, not likely to take place any time in the near future. Even Russia has not – at least initially – participated in all of the sessions at the summits, nor has it participated in all of the important preparatory work leading up to the summits, such as meetings of the G-7 finance ministers.

14. The Nordic UN Project. *The United Nations in Development. Reform Issues in the Economic and Social Fields. A Nordic Perspective*. Stockholm: Almqvist & Wiksell, 1991, p. 11; and The Commission on Global Governance. *Our Global Neighbourhood*. Oxford: Oxford University Press, 1995, pp. 153–162. See also: United Nations Development Programme. *Human Development Report*. New York: Oxford University Press, 1992, pp. 82–83.

15. Haq, Mahbub ul. *Reflections on Human Development*. New York: Oxford University Press, 1996, pp. 190–199.

16. International conferences that have addressed issues of particular concern to developing countries include, e.g., nine UN Conferences on Trade and Development, dating back to 1964. Other precursors to the global conferences of the 1990s include the UN Conference on the Human Environment (Stockholm, 1972) and the World Food Conference (Rome, 1974).

17. See also: Jolly, Richard. "Human Development: The World After Copenhagen". *Global Governance: A Review of Multilateralism and International Organizations* 3 (May–August) 1997, pp. 233–248.

18. This section on the evolution of the technical cooperation activities of the UN and the specialized agencies is primarily based on Kaufmann, Johann, Dick Leurdijk, and Nico Schrijver. *The World in Turmoil: Testing the UN's Capacity*. Hanover, NH: The Academic Council on the United Nations System, 1991, pp. 86–98.

19. The United Nations Children's Fund (UNICEF) was established in 1946 as the UN Children's Emergency Fund for countries ravaged by World War II. In 1953 UNICEF was set on a permanent footing by the General Assembly with a mandate to provide assistance to children in developing countries.

20. The mandate of the Special Fund did, however, go beyond that of the Expanded Programme on Technical Assistance and included support to pre-investment studies, research, and experimental projects. It took until 1960 before a global facility to provide loans on concessional terms to developing countries was created through the establishment of the International Development Association as part of the World Bank.

21. General Assembly Resolution 2688 (XXV). "The Capacity of the United Nations Development System". 11 December 1970. Often referred to as "The 1970 Consensus". Other key concepts introduced by the resolution included: provision of assistance through multi-year country programmes; and a tripartite partnership between recipient governments and the UNDP, who would jointly decide and monitor the use of the funds, and the specialized agencies, who would execute projects and provide necessary technical assistance.

22. New programmes established include the UN Population Fund (UNFPA), the UN Capital Development Fund (UNCDF), and the UN Drug Control Programme (UNDCP). World Bank technical assistance increased from a mere US$68 million in 1968 to US$1.5 billion in 1994. The sharpest increase took place in the 1970s. See document DP/1997/30/Add.1. "Information on United Nations System Regular and Extrabudgetary Technical Cooperation Expenditures Financed from Sources other than UNDP". 16 July 1997.

23. Report of the UN Secretary-General to the General Assembly A/50/202/

Add.1. "Comprehensive Statistical Data on Operational Activities for Development for the Year 1994". 25 September 1995; and the Organization for Economic Cooperation and Development, Development Assistance Committee. *Development Co-operation Report, 1995*. Paris: OECD, 1996.

24. General Assembly Resolutions 53/192, 50/120, 47/199, and 44/211. All entitled "Triennial Policy Review of Operational Activities for Development of the United Nations System". 25 February 1999, 16 February 1996, 22 December 1992, and 23 February 1990.

25. Economic and Social Council Resolution 849 (XXXII). "Use of Volunteer Workers in the Operational Programmes of the United Nations and Related Agencies Designed to Assist in the Economic and Social Development of the Less Developed Countries". 3 August 1961. The establishment of volunteer sending agencies in Europe, and in particular the Peace Corps, which was established in the United States in 1961, influenced the debate in ECOSOC and also contributed to the creation of a UN Volunteers programme. Many, however, consider missionaries as the first volunteers working for improved standards of living in developing countries, and "some of the best missionary values have continued to inspire the international volunteer movement" according to the UN Volunteers. "The Appropriate Use of Volunteers in Development". *United Nations Volunteers Thematic Series*, Programme Advisory Note. Geneva: UNV, 1991, p. 13

26. General Assembly Resolution 2659 (XXV) "United Nations Volunteers", 17 December 1970, established the UNV programme following among others General Assembly Resolution 2460 (XXIII) "Human Resources for Development", 20 December 1968, which requested ECOSOC to study the feasibility of creating an international corps of volunteers for development. Prior to 1994, the Executive Board was known as the Governing Council of the UNDP.

27. (a) General Assembly Resolution 31/166. "United Nations Volunteers". 14 February 1977; (b) UNDP Governing Council decision 90/34. "Fifth Programming Cycle". 23 June 1990; (c) UNDP Executive Board decision 94/14. "UNDP: Initiative for Change". 10 June 1994.

28. See Economic and Social Council Resolution 1444 (XLVII). "Utilization of Volunteers in United Nations Development Projects". 7 August 1969. Another possibility would have been to let the UN funds, programmes, and specialized agencies recruit their own volunteers, as they do with other international personnel for development projects. Since this, however, was not done, in effect, a monopoly was created for the recruitment and administration of volunteers for UN development cooperation projects.

29. Note by the Secretary-General to the Economic and Social Council E/4663. "Utilization of Volunteers in United Nations Development Projects". 16 May 1969.

30. General Assembly Resolution 2460 (XXIII). "Human Resources for Development". 20 December 1968.

31. (a) General Assembly Resolution 40/212. "International Volunteers Day". 17 December 1985; (b) General Assembly Resolution 52/17. "International Year of Volunteers, 2001". 20 November 1997.

32. The figures quoted in this paragraph and subsequent paragraphs describing the evolution of the programme are taken from a series of annual publications by the United Nations Volunteers entitled: *UNV at a Glance – The Key Statistics*. Geneva: UNV, 1990–1996, including the latest in the series: *UNV at a Glance – The Key Statistics*. Bonn: UNV, 1997–1998.

33. Report of the Secretary-General to the General Assembly A/50/202/Add.1. "Comprehensive Statistical Data on Operational Activities for Development for the Year 1994". 25 September 1995.

34. The UN Department of Economic and Social Affairs includes what was previously known as the UN Department of Development Support and Management Services (UNDDSMS), a successor to the UN Department of Technical Cooperation for Development (UNDTCD).

35. See: General Assembly Resolution 31/131. "United Nations Volunteers Programme". 7 February 1977.

36. Compared to 1989, when the ratio of male to female Volunteers was 4:1, the programme has made some progress in increasing the number of female Volunteers. This paragraph and subsequent ones continue to draw on the annual publications: *UNV at a Glance – The Key Statistics*. Geneva: United Nations Volunteers, 1990, and subsequent updates, including: *UNV at a Glance – The Key Statistics for 1997*. Bonn: UNV, 1998.

37. In 1989, the average cost for a UNV specialist was US$20,300, and US$6,000 for a UNV community worker, while the administrative cost per Volunteer was US$4,700. This means that the average costs of UNV specialists have increased by 58 per cent between 1989 and 1996, while average costs of UNV community workers and administrative costs increased by 15 and 17 per cent, respectively, during the same period.

38. Wilson, Irene and Marjon Nooter, eds. *Evaluation of Finnish Personnel as Volunteers in Development Cooperation*, Ministry for Foreign Affairs of Finland, Department for International Development Cooperation, Report 1995:3. Helsinki: Hakapaino, 1995, pp. 204–206.

39. United Nations Volunteers. *Volunteers against Conflict*. Tokyo: United Nations University Press, 1996, p. 225.

3

Focus

An assessment of an intergovernmental organization such as the UN, or even part of it, presents a number of methodological difficulties and several potential dangers. These include an oversimplification of the issues to be analysed, reductionism, and resorting to balance sheet-type approaches or very crude cost-benefit analyses. Any programme of the UN, consequently, needs to be assessed using the right yardstick, appropriate criteria, and suitable indicators, which are based on the mandate of the programme and the nature of its activities.[1]

In this study, accordingly, the substantive focus of the assessment has been determined first, after which the approach and conceptual framework of the study were designed. The methodology of the study is based on a review of previous studies by the UN and other volunteer sending agencies as well as more general evaluation literature.

Research questions and focus of the study

The primary purpose of this study is to assess one programme of the UN, the UN Volunteers (UNV) programme, in terms of its impact. The impact of the programme refers to the achievement of the overall objectives of the programme. In addition, the study assesses the perceived value of the programme to its users and beneficiaries. The study examines the UNV programme in one country, Nepal, and covers a 10-year period, from 1987 to 1996.[2]

The broader purpose of the evaluation of the UNV programme is to serve as a case study of the impact of the development cooperation activities of the UN, understood as the extent to which a UN programme achieves its objectives and produces desired outcomes. The study also attempts to demonstrate a methodology that could be used to assess other UN funds, programmes, and agencies.

The specific focus of the study is on answering two questions.

1. Does the UNV programme have any impact?
2. What is the perceived value of the programme to its users and beneficiaries?

In trying to answer these questions, the study addresses six specific issues, the first three of which relate to the impact of the programme, and the latter three of which relate to the perceived value of the programme:

1. changes in human capital
2. changes in social capital
3. changes in job opportunities, poverty, women's lives, and the environment
4. the relevance of the work of the Volunteers
5. the performance of the Volunteers
6. the results and sustainability of the work of the Volunteers.

In addition to these six main objectives, the study also includes an assessment of the performance of the headquarters of the UNV programme and of benefits to the Volunteers of participating in the programme.

Human capital

The UNV programme was originally established to supply trained manpower to developing countries, to transfer skills and knowledge, and to fill gaps in human resources that were perceived to be lacking in the developing countries. An assessment of the programme should therefore review the achievements of the programme with respect to human resource development – or what could be referred to as changes in human capital – in developing countries.[3]

The interest in human resource development as a way to promote economic development can be traced back to a general theory of investments in human capital which was developed by Theodore W. Schultz and Gary S. Becker in the late 1950s and early 1960s. According to Becker and other proponents of the human capital theory, investments in human capital – that is, education and training – improve the skills, knowledge, or health of people, increase their productivity, and raise their monetary or non-monetary income.[4]

The basic assumption that an investment in human capital leads to an increase in labour productivity has been questioned by many critics of human capital theory. Evidence supporting the link between human capital and economic growth does, however, remain strong, even if research until recently seems to have added very little new, except confirm the theory.[5]

Empirical research regarding the economic development of several East Asian countries suggests a strong link between education and economic growth, and a pay-off to investments in human capital. Analyses of the remarkable economic development of a number of countries during the past 40 years – most notably Japan, followed by Hong Kong, Singapore, South Korea and Taiwan – argue that at least part of their success in terms of achieving economic growth, and social progress, can be attributed to investments in human capital, that is, education and training. Other vital ingredients to growth often mentioned in the East Asian context include high savings rates, low taxes and low government spending, flexible labour markets, and openness to trade.[6]

Even if disagreement does exist as to how much of the economic growth in East Asia really can be attributed to increases in productivity, and how much can be explained by a heavy investment in capital and a movement of labour from a less productive agrarian sector to a more productive industrial sector, little disagreement seems to exist regarding the importance of education and training to economic growth – the fundamental issue of relevance to this study.[7]

Supported by research findings such as the ones pertaining to East Asia, human resource development once again came to the forefront of the development discussion in the 1990s. During much of the 1970s and the 1980s, human resource development was overshadowed by other development paradigms, the debt crises, and the perceived need for structural adjustment in developing countries as a precondition for development. Increasingly since the early 1990s, however, people are once again viewed as both the means as well as the end of economic development. Human development has emerged as a leading paradigm, according to which the purpose of development is to enlarge people's choices – whether economic, social, cultural, or political. Investments in human resource development, in turn, become an important means for human development.[8]

Two conclusions can be drawn from this recent history: the first is that human resource development remains a relevant focus of development cooperation, and the second is that if human capital accumulation can be shown to result from a UN programme, it can be asserted that the programme has contributed to economic development. For this to hold for the UNV programme, it would require being able to demonstrate that new skills or knowledge have been acquired by people who have been trained by or worked with the UN Volunteers. Proving, or disproving, this is the first objective of this study.

Social capital

In 1977, the mandate of the UNV programme was expanded to include support to the participation of people and communities in the development process. An assessment of the programme should therefore also ascertain the contribution of the programme in these areas, or what could be labelled social capital formation.[9]

In general, social capital refers to, or is manifested in, features such as cooperation and civic engagement in a society or community. Like other forms of capital, social capital is productive and enables the achievement of certain objectives that would not be attainable in its absence. Social capital promotes cooperative behavior instead of uncooperative behavior, as game theory would predict, and improves the performance of a society or a community by facilitating coordinated actions.[10]

A society or community that possesses social capital is characterized by notions of cooperation and reciprocity that bind people together, solidarity, trust, and tolerance, and active participation in public affairs. In a way this can be seen as "enlightened self-interest", with the aim of increasing the benefits for everyone. Where social capital exists, a variety of civic associations and non-governmental organizations can usually be found.[11]

The effect of social capital on economic development is a fairly recent area of study, the number of studies on the subject are few, and the theory is still under development. However, the appropriateness of studying the contribution of a UN programme towards social capital accumulation should not depend on whether or not there is a link between social capital and economic development.[12]

Considering that social capital is a rather recent area of research, studying the subject may contribute to the development of the theory and methodology of the subject area. Moreover, at a time when there are increasing calls for the involvement of civil society in the work of the UN, it is particularly relevant to assess the work of the UN with civil society organizations and the effect of the UN Volunteers on the values, attitudes, motivation, participation, and cooperation of people in the communities or organizations where Volunteers worked. This thus becomes the second objective of this study.[13]

Jobs, poverty, women, and the environment

From the debates of the Governing Council of the UNDP in the late 1980s and its successor, the Executive Board, in the early 1990s, four areas of focus emerged for the organization: jobs, poverty, women, and the environment. Since the majority of the UN Volunteers were working on UNDP projects during the period covered by this study (1987–96), it also seems appropriate to assess the effect of the UNV programme on job opportunities, the level of poverty, the status of women, and the environment in the areas of Nepal where the Volunteers worked. This is the third objective of this study.[14]

Perceived value of the programme

In addition to the impact of the UNV programme, this study also assesses the perceived value of the programme to former supervisors and co-workers of the Volunteers and other beneficiaries of the work of the Volunteers.

The fourth objective of the study is to assess the relevance of the work of the Volunteers. The fifth objective of the study is to evaluate the performance of the Volunteers compared to other alternatives – volunteers from other organizations, UN experts, other expatriates, and nationals of the country where the Volunteers served, who conceivably could have been hired to do the same job as the UN Volunteers. The sixth objective of the study is to assess the results of the activities initiated by the Volunteers, their continuation, and their long-term benefits.[15]

Literature review

Studies by the United Nations

Only one comprehensive attempt to review the UNV programme has been carried out since the inception of the programme. This took place in 1987 at the request of the UNDP Governing Council, to which a report was submitted the following year. The review discusses the concept and mandate of the UN Volunteers, and addresses a number of management issues, financing, staffing of the head office, recruitment and training of Volunteers, and programming of Volunteer inputs.[16]

The evaluation is based on several different sources of data and covers several countries, but does not address the most relevant issues of this study: the outcomes of the work of the UN Volunteers and the perceived value of the programme to the beneficiaries of the programme. The study contains general views of users and administrators of the programme, but does not include actual assessments of the work of individual Volunteers.

The same very general nature characterizes the information in the other approximately 90 evaluations and reviews that have been carried out from 1987 to 1996 on specific projects or activities of the UN Volunteers. This is the major shortcoming in these evaluation reports, which are listed in Appendix C. The evaluations mainly focus on the implementation of activities of UN Volunteers and ways of improving the programme. While these studies do suggest factors that could be included in a framework to study the perceived value of the UNV programme, the previous evaluations have little to offer in terms of substance or methodology for an assessment of the impact of the programme.

A number of other development projects without UN Volunteers have also been funded and evaluated by the UNDP. For the purposes of this study, the most interesting evaluations are the ones that deal with human resource development and strengthening of institutions in developing countries, often referred to as "capacity building".

Two things become clear from a review of the past UNDP studies: the first thing is that the studies contain little in terms of impact of UNDP supported activities; the second thing is that there is little in terms of methodology that the previous UNDP evaluations could offer an assessment of the impact of the UNV programme, even if the UNDP Evaluation Office in recent years has begun to emphasize the need to assess the impact of UNDP supported programmes and projects.[17]

A reason that previous UNDP studies have little to offer an impact assessment is that during the last 20 years, the design and implementation of projects, rather than their outcomes and long-term benefits, have been the primary concern of evaluations of the UNDP, the World Bank, and other development agencies. This can, at least in part, be seen as a reaction to the limited utility of several large-scale impact evaluations that were conducted in the 1970s.[18]

Despite a realization as early as 1988 that better data was needed to be able to assess the impact of UNDP projects, many UNDP human resource development and capacity building projects have failed to specify in sufficient detail who the beneficiaries of these projects are, which makes an assessment of their impact difficult.[19]

In the past, a key component of many UNDP projects was to provide overseas and on-the-job training to individuals working in government ministries and departments. The underlying assumption was that the training would strengthen the capacity of these institutions to carry out their functions, which would benefit a large number of, unspecified, people in the whole country. This approach, even if based on a valid assumption, makes it difficult to measure any impact, and may also explain the inability of the UNDP and the UNV to assess the impact of their activities.

This does, however, also provide the methodological entry point for this study: to identify and locate the individuals who have been trained by the UN Volunteers, and to assess the benefits of the training provided to them. Even if records of beneficiaries are poor or non-existent, it should be possible to identify beneficiaries of UNV assistance by visiting institutions or communities where the Volunteers have worked. If beneficiaries cannot be found, or traced anywhere else, the conclusion that would have to be drawn is that there has not been any lasting impact.

UN Volunteers may in some ways be a distinct group, but the same methodology could equally well be used for personnel from any of the other UN agencies who have provided on-the-job training as part of their assignment with FAO, ILO, UNESCO, UNIDO, WHO, another specialized agency, or a department of the UN. The methodology could also be used to assess the impact of training abroad, and be adapted to measure the perceived value of other

inputs provided to strengthen national institutions and human resources in developing countries. In this way, the methodology used
in this study could be used to assess the work of several other UN
programmes, funds, and agencies and respond to the request by the
UNDP Governing Council in 1988 for the development of a methodology to assess the impact of human resource development projects
on economic development.[20]

Despite, or perhaps because of, the limited focus on impact evaluations in the last 20 years, there is again a great deal of interest in
the assessment of the impact of the work of the UN. At the request
of the General Assembly, an evaluation of the impact of the UN
supported development cooperation activities was carried out in
1997–98. The overarching theme of the evaluation is capacity
building, which encompasses strengthening of institutions and
human resources and is therefore very relevant to this study.[21]

The UN evaluation deals with how the funds, programmes, and
agencies of the UN system have worked together in trying to build
national capacities. The scope of the UN evaluation is, therefore,
much broader than the scope of this study. The UN evaluation
relies on existing data and reports as well as expert judgements and
does therefore not provide any methodological insights to this
study, except that it also looks at how objective indicators of economic development have changed during a period when the UN
system provided assistance to a country. UN support to the health
sector over a period of 15 years, for instance, is related against
changes in national health indicators such as life expectancy and
infant mortality.[22]

The UN impact evaluation, which was a first attempt to assess the
impact of the operational activities of the UN on a system-wide
basis, consists of six separate country studies. The studies suggest
that the UN system has had a positive impact on capacity building,
and the conclusion of the six case studies is that these provide the
basis for more in-depth analysis of the impact of the UN using a
larger sample and more refined techniques. The need to continue
evaluations of the impact of the work of the UN at country level was

noted by the member states of the UN, who welcomed the impact evaluation.[23]

While this may not have been the case until the early 1990s, impact evaluations of projects and programmes are now standard practice of the World Bank. Impact evaluations are conducted several years after the completion of a project or a programme to assess any lasting contribution by the World Bank to the development of a borrower country. Although World Bank projects and programmes are very different from the activities of the UNV programme, the World Bank experience of impact evaluations is definitely also relevant to an assessment of the impact of the UNV programme.[24]

A starting point for the World Bank impact evaluations is to try to provide a reasonable coverage of the impact on the beneficiaries as well as the impact on groups that may have been negatively affected and other stakeholders in the project or programme. The specific methodology itself may differ between different evaluations, depending on the nature of the project or programme. In many cases sample surveys are used to collect the necessary data, in other cases, focus groups or structured interviews with key informants may be considered sufficient.

The World Bank defines the total impact of a project or a programme as the sum of intended effects as well as any side-effects that can reasonably be attributed to the project or programme concerned. To attribute effects to a specific project or programme, an explicit intervention model is used, which is based on a logical framework that links inputs to outputs, outcomes, and ultimately the impact of the World Bank assistance.

The basic criterion for resolving the attribution question is to compare a situation with and without the World Bank project or programme concerned. Simply comparing the situation before and after the World Bank intervention, without a control comparator that is unaffected by the intervention, may not be correct because some of the effects may have occurred independently of the intervention.

As the experience of the World Bank shows, however, it is in practice often difficult to define a situation with and without the intervention. This is particularly the case without good baseline data at the outset and a monitoring and evaluation system generating adequate observations over time in the project or programme areas and similarly situated control areas. Sometimes, the only choice for constructing a "counterfactual scenario" (i.e., a situation without the project or programme) may be to extrapolate trends to approximate the situation without the project or programme.

Research by other volunteer sending agencies

Information was requested, but little was received, from other volunteer sending agencies, including one of the oldest and biggest, the Peace Corps in the US.[25] This may be due to the fact that little research on the impact of these other volunteer agencies has been carried out. This in itself is not surprising, since volunteer programmes almost by definition try to be low-cost and evaluations can be expensive undertakings. A Canadian study does, however, exist that assesses the benefits of the Canadian volunteer sending programmes to Canada and the Canadians, but the study does not look at the benefits to the countries receiving volunteers.[26]

A summary of the experiences of some European volunteer agencies is included in an evaluation of the Finnish volunteer programme.[27] Again, very little can be found in this overview on the achievements of these bilateral volunteer programmes. Instead, general statements are made regarding the appreciation by host organizations in developing countries of the volunteers, their motivation, commitment, and technical expertise. As was the case with many UNDP-funded projects, it may be that the beneficiaries of these programmes have not been adequately specified for evaluators to be able to identify beneficiaries and interview them about the impact of the programmes.[28]

Other literature consulted and methods considered

According to much of the general evaluation literature, an assessment of the impact of development cooperation activities should use randomized or quasi-experimental evaluation designs.[29] Results of studies using these methods have, however, been disappointing, and unable to provide policy makers, planners, or managers with the information they need. An increasing number of researchers are therefore arguing that these studies are too complex, time-consuming, and expensive, and that more rapid and economical ways of obtaining the desired information should be used. If simpler and more economical designs are used, two common features of quasi-experimental designs should, however, be incorporated or compensated for to the extent possible: (i) measurement before and after an intervention and (ii) the use of a control group.[30]

Of the different possible methods available to estimate the effects of the UNV programme in terms of human capital accumulation, measuring changes in the productivity of individuals who have been trained by UN Volunteers, and comparing these with changes in productivity among those who received no training from the Volunteers but who otherwise were similar, would seem to be a suitable approach.[31]

Many productivity studies have found that individuals with different levels of education and training generally perform different kinds of jobs, particularly in the non-farm sectors, where the main pay-off for additional education and training is an opportunity to move into higher paying jobs.[32] If this is true, the reverse should also be true, and it should be possible to use movement into better paying jobs, promotions, added responsibility, etc., as indicators of changes in the productivity of individuals. This, it seems, could be used to assess the outcomes of the work of the UN Volunteers.

However, using productivity comparisons would not be easy or appropriate, since very few individuals have been trained by UN Volunteers for clearly defined or prolonged periods of time. Consequently, it would be very difficult to attribute movement into better jobs to the training provided by the UN Volunteers, even if one used a control group to eliminate the influence of factors other than the training provided by the Volunteers. Another dilemma is that most UN Volunteers have worked with government institutions and non-profit organizations, where changes in productivity are even more difficult to measure.

United Nations University Press
53-70, Jingumae 5-chome
Shibuya-ku, Tokyo 150-8925
Japan

Reader's Reply Card

TITLE:

Author/Editor:

The information on this card will help us to improve our publishing programme. Please complete the card and return it to the United Nations University Press.

Name

What are your areas of interest?

Development.	☐
Social Sciences.	☐

Address

Natural Resources.	☐
Economics	☐
Food and Nutrition	☐
Energy.	☐
International Law	☐

Country

Politics	☐
Culture.	☐
Science and Technology.	☐
Other.	☐

☐ ☐ ☐ ☐ ☐

How did you come to know about this book?

UNU Press Publications Catalogue	
Advertisement in.	
Distributor	
Bookstore	
Other.	

I am interested in information about the UNU . . . . ☐

Please add my name to the catalogue mailing list. . . . . . . ☐

In light of the above, using productivity comparisons clearly poses some problems. Moreover, even if it would be possible to use changes in productivity as a measure of the impact of the UNV programme in terms of human capital accumulation, it would still be necessary to find other, preferably similar, observable indicators to measure the other objectives of the study. This would be even more difficult for social capital accumulation and the effect of the work of the Volunteers on jobs, poverty, women's lives, and the environment.

A better alternative, therefore, was to devise a methodology that allowed for an assessment of all of the objectives of the study at the same time, within the same theoretical framework. Even if the ideal might have been to find observable indicators for measuring the impact of the UNV programme, basing an assessment on the perceptions of the users and beneficiaries of the programme is also a valid approach. The opinion of the people themselves of how their lives have changed is often as valuable as an assessment of observable indicators of change.[33]

Notes

1. Roberts, Adam and Benedict Kingsbury, "The UN's Roles in International Society since 1945". In: Roberts, Adam and Benedict Kingsbury, eds. *United Nations, Divided World*, 2nd edn. New York: Oxford University Press, 1993, pp. 14–17.
2. The criteria on which the assessment of the UNV programme are based and the definitions used have been derived from several different sources, including: (a) the Organization for Economic Cooperation and Development. *Principles for Evaluation of Development Assistance*, Development Assistance Committee, OCDE/GD 208. Paris: OECD, 1991; (b) the United Nations Development Programme. *Results-oriented Monitoring and Evaluation*, Office of Evaluation and Strategic Planning, UNDP/OESP. New York: UNDP, 1997, pp. 25–27; (c) The International Labour Office. *Guidelines for the Preparation of Independent Evaluations of ILO Programmes and Projects*, Evaluation Unit, ILO, PROG/EVAL. Geneva: ILO, 1997, pp. 3–4.
3. General Assembly Resolution 2659 (XXV). "United Nations Volunteers". 17 December 1970.
4. See: (a) Blaug, Mark. *The Methodology of Economics: Or How Economists Explain*, 2nd edn. Cambridge, UK: Cambridge University Press, 1994, p. 206; (b) Becker, Gary S. *Human Capital: A Theoretical and Empirical Approach with Special*

Reference to Education. New York: The Columbia University Press for NBER, 1964 (Chicago: The University of Chicago Press, 1993, reprint).

5. See: (a) Barro, Robert J. and Xavier Sala-i-Martin. *Economic Growth*. New York: McGraw-Hill, 1995; and (b) for a complementary view Blaug, Mark. *The Methodology of Economics: Or How Economists Explain*, 2nd edn. Cambridge, UK: Cambridge University Press, 1994, pp. 206–219.

6. World Bank. *The East Asian Miracle: Economic Growth and Public Policy*. New York: Oxford University Press, 1993. The economic difficulties that the East Asian countries faced in the late 1990s should not detract from the extraordinary economic development of these countries over the past 40 years.

7. Krugman, Paul. "The Myth of the Asian Miracle". *Foreign Affairs* 73 (November–December), pp. 62–78, 1994. See also: (a) "The Asian Economic Miracle". *UBS International Finance*, No. 29 (Autumn 1996); (b) Michael Sarel. "Growth and Productivity in ASEAN Economies", paper presented at an IMF conference in Jakarta, Indonesia. November 1996.

8. Haq, Mahbub ul. *Reflections on Human Development*. New York: Oxford University Press, 1996, pp. 3–23. See also: United Nations Development Programme. *Human Development Report*. New York: Oxford University Press, 1996.

9. General Assembly Resolution 31/166. "United Nations Volunteers". 14 February 1977.

10. See: (a) Putnam, Robert. *Making Democracy Work: Civic Traditions in Modern Italy*. Princeton, NJ: Princeton University Press, 1993, pp. 163–176; (b) Coleman, James S. *Foundations of Social Theory*. Cambridge, MA: Harvard University Press, 1990, pp. 300–321.

11. Putnam, Robert. *Making Democracy Work: Civic Traditions in Modern Italy*. Princeton, NJ: Princeton University Press, 1993, pp. 86–91.

12. See also *1997 World Development Report*. Washington, DC: Oxford University Press for the World Bank, 1997, pp. 114–116, for a discussion on the contribution of social capital to economic development.

13. Regarding the need to assess issues such as the promotion of participation or the encouragement of self-reliant strategies, see Marsden, David and Peter Oakley, eds. *Evaluating Social Development Projects*, Development Guidelines 5. Oxford: Oxfam, 1990.

14. (a) UNDP Governing Council decision 89/20. "The Role of the United Nations Development Programme in the 1990s". 30 June 1989; (b) UNDP Governing Council decision 90/34. "Fifth Programming Cycle". 23 June 1990; (c) UNDP Executive Board decision 94/14. "UNDP: Initiative for Change". 10 June 1994.

15. In addition to references cited earlier, the criteria for the assessment of the perceived value of the UNV programme also draw on: (a) United Nations Administrative Committee on Coordination. *Monitoring and Evaluation: Guiding Principles*. Rome: IFAD Publications, 1985; (b) United Nations Children's Fund. *Making a Difference: A UNICEF Guide to Monitoring and Evaluation*. New York: UNICEF, 1991. For a discussion on the concept and importance of sustainability, see: Valadez, Joseph and Michael Bamberger, eds. *Monitoring and Evaluating Social Programmes in Developing Countries*, EDI Development Studies. Washington, DC: The World Bank, 1994, pp. 183–188.

16. (a) UNDP Governing Council decision 87/36. "United Nations Volunteers". 19 June 1987; (b) Report of the Administrator to the UNDP Governing Council DP/1988/46/Add.1. "Review of the United Nations Volunteers". 23 March 1988.

17. United Nations Development Programme. (a) *Guidelines for Evaluators*, UNDP/OESP. New York: UNDP, 1993; (b) *Evaluation Findings in 1994–1995; Evaluation Findings in 1996*, UNDP/OESP. New York: UNDP, 1996; 1997.

18. Valadez, Joseph and Michael Bamberger, eds. *Monitoring and Evaluating Social Programmes in Developing Countries*, EDI Development Studies. Washington, DC: The World Bank, 1994, p. 28, p. 227.

19. In 1988, following a review of the UNDP's experience in human resource development, the UNDP Governing Council requested that a methodology to measure the impact of human resource development projects on social and economic development be developed. However, this apparently never materialized. See: (a) Report of the Administrator to the UNDP Governing Council DP/1988/62. "Experience in Human Resource Development since 1970". 15 March 1988; (b) UNDP Governing Council decision 88/29. "Experience in Human Resource Development". 1 July 1988.

20. UNDP Governing Council decision 88/29. "Experience in Human Resource Development". 1 July 1988.

21. General Assembly Resolution 50/120. "Triennial Policy Review of Operational Activities for Development of the United Nations System". 16 February 1996, paragraph 56.

22. Report by the Secretary General to the Economic and Social Council E/1997/65. "Progress in the Implementation of General Assembly Resolution 50/120". 11 June 1997, paragraphs 77–81, contain a brief description of the methodology and areas covered by the study.

23. (a) General Assembly Document A/53/226. "Triennial Policy Review of Operational Activities for Development of the United Nations System". 12 August 1998, paragraphs 18–35; (b) General Assembly Resolution 53/192. "Triennial Policy Review of Operational Activities for Development of the United Nations System". 25 February 1999, paragraph 53.

24. World Bank. "Evaluating Development Operations: Methods for Judging Outcomes and Impacts". Operations Evaluation Department. *Lessons & Practices.* number 10 (July), pp. 4–5, 1997.

25. The establishment of the Peace Corps in 1961 is often viewed as the birth of volunteer programmes to support development cooperation. The creation of the Peace Corps certainly gave a boost to the institutionalization and growth of volunteer programmes to support development and also contributed to the establishment of the UNV programme. Other programmes, however, did predate the Peace Corps, such as the British Voluntary Services Overseas, which was established in 1958.

26. Strategic Planning Associates and C.A.C. International. "Effects of Canadian Volunteer Sending". Ottawa, 1994.

27. Wilson, Irene and Marjon Nooter, eds. *Evaluation of Finnish Personnel as Volunteers in Development Cooperation*, Ministry for Foreign Affairs of Finland,

Department for International Development Cooperation, Report 1995:3. Helsinki: Hakapaino, 1995, pp. 29–45.

28. In addition to the well-established North American and European volunteer agencies, a number of volunteer sending organizations have in recent years also been established in several countries in Asia, Africa, and Latin America, but no evaluations of these programmes could be found.

29. (a) Cook, Thomas H. and Donald T. Campbell. *Quasi Experimentation: Design and Analysis Issues for Field Setting.* Boston: Houghton-Mifflin, 1979; (b) Boruch, Robert F. and Werner Wothke, eds. *Randomization and Field Experimentation.* San Francisco: Jossey-Bass, 1985.

30. Valadez, Joseph and Michael Bamberger, eds. *Monitoring and Evaluating Social Programmes in Developing Countries*, EDI Development Studies. Washington, DC: The World Bank, 1994, p. 228.

31. Ways of studying investments in human capital and, more generally, the relationship between education, training, and economic development, include cost-benefit analysis to calculate an internal rate of return, growth accounting methods, productivity studies, correlation studies, regression analysis, and other econometric methods.

32. See: Psacharopoulos, George and Maureen Woodhall. *Education for Development. An Analysis of Investment Choices.* Washington, DC: Oxford University Press for the World Bank, 1985, pp. 46–53.

33. Valadez, Joseph and Michael Bamberger, eds. *Monitoring and Evaluating Social Programmes in Developing Countries*, EDI Development Studies. Washington, DC: The World Bank, 1994, p. 313.

4

Methodology

Approach

Approaches tested

A first attempt to assess the impact of the UNV programme was made by analysing the contents of the reports prepared by the Volunteers themselves on their assignments. The review covered 30 countries in Africa, Asia, the Pacific, Latin America, the Caribbean, the Middle East, and Europe. Unfortunately, even if a report should have been completed by each Volunteer, in many cases either a report had not been submitted, had been misplaced and could not be found, or had been submitted but was incomplete.[1]

In the case of Nepal, for instance, reports could be retrieved for only 59 of the 110 UN Volunteer assignments that had been completed during the period covered by the study (1987–96). This corresponds to 54 per cent, which was not considered a sufficient basis for an analysis of the impact of the UNV programme.[2]

Another even more serious problem with the review of the reports of the Volunteers as an approach is that little relevant information on the outcomes of the work of the Volunteers could be found in the reports. The reports address many other issues, particularly of an administrative nature, but they contain little on what has been achieved by the Volunteers. Still, a review of a total of 562 reports was completed. The information contained in the reports was used to get an overview of the extent to which different kinds of training had been performed by the Volunteers, and the kinds of skills and knowledge that had been transferred by the Volunteers.

Another way to try to assess the impact of the UNV programme was to review almost 90 evaluation reports and assessments of the activities of the UN Volunteers that were available for the period covered by the study. An attempt was made to use meta-analysis to synthesize the findings of the 88 evaluations and reviews shown in Appendix C.[3]

Meta-analysis was considered an appropriate approach to try to assess the impact of the UNV programme since the evaluation reports covered a fairly representative sample of the activities of the UNV programme from different countries during the period covered by the study. What could not be anticipated was how little the evaluation reports contain in terms of results or impact of the work of the Volunteers. Predominantly, the reports are what could be described as input focused, process oriented, and problem centred.[4]

Some of the evaluation reports do contain examples of results of the work of the Volunteers, such as high pass rates of students taught by UNV teachers or improvements in the living conditions of the beneficiaries, but these examples are few and far between. Most of the reports only describe the activities of the Volunteers, such as the provision of on-the-job training or the introduction of income-generating activities, but do not describe the results of these activities. None of the evaluations specifically looked at the impact of the activities of the Volunteers some time after the Volunteers had left.

What the reports do contain, and what could be used in this study, was information about issues that had affected the work of the Volunteers, usually negatively. These issues were included in the conceptual framework of the study. Beyond that, the reports provided little except general views of government and UN officials on the work of the UN Volunteers and the performance of the head office of the programme, and nothing or very little on the perceived value of the programme to the beneficiaries. What became clear was that it would be necessary to collect original data to be able to assess the impact of the UNV programme and its perceived value to the users and beneficiaries of the programme.

Methodology adopted

Even if the review of the reports prepared by the Volunteers and the evaluation reports yielded little information about actual results of the work of the Volunteers, these reviews provided the basis for the development of a survey to assess the impact of the UNV programme. Based on these reviews and the reports prepared by the Volunteers, a number of factors that could explain the outcomes of the work of the Volunteers were identified, and an inventory of issues to be included in a survey was developed.

The next step included interviews with government officials, representatives of non-governmental organizations, supervisors and co-workers of Volunteers, and beneficiaries of the UNV programme, in order to sharpen the focus of the study and to anticipate potential problems with the research design. The preliminary interviews were carried out during visits to Nepal, India, Bhutan, and Costa Rica.[5]

Following these exploratory visits, a decision was made to collect data through a mail survey addressed to former Volunteers and through interviews with individuals who had worked with or benefited from the work of the Volunteers. This included co-workers and supervisors of the Volunteers, and representatives of UN agencies, government departments, civil society organizations, and communities where UN Volunteers had worked. It was also decided to introduce a reference group in the study, in order to compare changes that could be attributed to the work of the Volunteers to changes that had taken place without any involvement of the Volunteers, that is, a "counterfactual situation".

During the exploratory visits it became clear that it would be impossible to identify respondents who in all other respects were similar to the users and beneficiaries of the programmes other than that they had not had any contact with the Volunteers. This was the reason that a control group, in the strict sense of the term, could not be introduced. The second-best, therefore, was to establish a refer-

Figure 4.1   Schematic illustration of the approach adopted

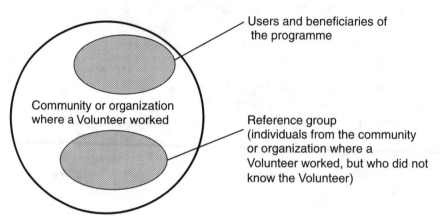

Users and beneficiaries of the programme

Community or organization where a Volunteer worked

Reference group
(individuals from the community or organization where a Volunteer worked, but who did not know the Volunteer)

ence group consisting of respondents who did not know a particular Volunteer, but who knew the community or organization where the Volunteer had worked. The role of the reference group was to describe changes that had taken place in the communities or organizations during the time the Volunteer had worked there. A schematic illustration of the approach adopted can be seen in Figure 4.1.

The approach adopted entailed collecting information from specific communities and organizations where a Volunteer had worked. On the one hand, information was collected from individuals who had either personally benefited from the work of Volunteers or otherwise been in direct contact with the Volunteers (users and beneficiaries), and on the other hand, information was collected from individuals who had had no contact whatsoever with the Volunteers (reference group). In addition, information was collected from former UN Volunteers themselves.

Selection of Nepal as a case study

During exploratory visits to Nepal (November 1995), India (December 1995), Costa Rica (December 1995), and Bhutan (April 1996), the appropriateness of each country as a case study was also assessed. The criteria used to determine which country or countries to select as case studies included: (i) the size of the Volunteers programme in the country; (ii) the availability of different categories of Volunteers; (iii) the variety in the assignments of the Volunteers; (iv) the role of the country as a host as well as supplier of Volunteers; and (v) the availability of surveyors to carry out the data collection for the study.

India was considered a potentially interesting case study because both international and national UN Volunteers had worked in the country and many Indians had worked abroad as Volunteers during the period covered by the study. However, the number of Volunteers who had served in India during this time, 44, was considered too small to justify selecting the country as a case study.

Similarly, the total number of volunteers who had served in Costa Rica between 1987 and 1996, 26, was considered too small, even if both international and national Volunteers had worked there. In contrast, Bhutan had one of the largest UNV programmes in the world, 250 international Volunteers between 1987 and 1996, and would have been suitable from the point of view of the size of the programme. However, the overall development context of the country was considered too special to make it suitable as a case study.

Nepal, on the other hand, was considered appropriate as a case study taking into consideration not only the length of the programme, which started in the mid 1970s, but also the size and availability of different categories of Volunteers in the country. During the period covered by the study, 97 international Volunteers, 50 UNV specialists and 47 UNV community workers, worked in Nepal. In 1987, the number of Volunteers working in Nepal was 25. During the late 1980s and early 1990s, the number of Volunteers grew and in 1991 the number reached 50, only to drop to 35 the following year and decline further to 30 in 1995. In 1996, another big drop brought the number of international Volunteers to 13. Meanwhile, national Volunteers were introduced in Nepal, with between 16 and 27 serving each year from 1993 to 1996 (see Fig. 4.2).

The fact that almost 350 Nepalese nationals served as Volunteers in other countries during this time also made Nepal attractive as a

**Figure 4.2   Number of Volunteers serving in Nepal by year
(1987–96)**

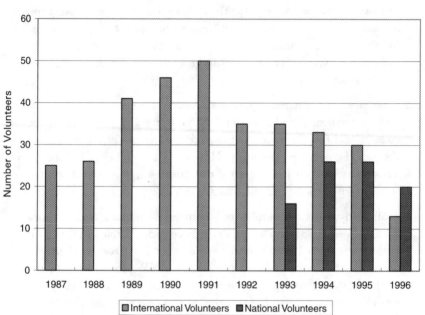

case study, even if this aspect of the programme was not analysed in
the end. Finally, it was also possible to identify and train a group of
interviewers to collect data in Nepal at a reasonable cost.

The idea of using more than one case study was seriously considered, but in the end rejected in order to be able to go into sufficient
depth in analysing the data from Nepal. Information and data from
other countries visited during the course of the study was instead
used to validate the methodology used and the results from Nepal.

Conceptual framework

At the time of the study, the UNV programme did not have an explicit model to explain how resources and activities were expected to

produce specific outcomes. A conceptual framework was therefore developed to analyse how the results were expected to be achieved. This was done using information obtained from reports and interview results, and by drawing on general evaluation literature and several different fields of study, including economics, organizational theory, sociology, anthropology, and political science.[6]

The outcome variables in the conceptual framework were derived from the six specific objectives of the study:

1. the impact of the programme in terms of human capital
2. the impact of the programme in terms of social capital
3. the impact of the programme in terms of changes in job opportunities, poverty, women's lives, and the environment
4. the perceived value of the programme in terms of the relevance of the work of the Volunteers
5. the perceived value of the programme in terms of the performance of the Volunteers
6. the perceived value of the programme in terms of the results and sustainability of the work of the Volunteers.

Even if the UNV programme may not have worked with explicit theoretical assumptions to guide its work at the time of the study, guidelines for the use of Volunteers in development cooperation did exist. These guidelines were used as a starting point for identifying factors or variables that could explain different outcomes.[7]

A logical framework was another starting point for the conceptual model of the study, based on the fact that most of the projects on which the Volunteers worked were designed using a logical framework.[8] The logical framework links the design of a project to its implementation by requiring the specification of inputs and activities that are expected to produce outputs and outcomes. A logical framework also identifies important assumptions and includes verifiable indicators of success, and may therefore help explain if an outcome was not achieved because the right kinds of inputs were not provided, or because important assumptions were not satisfied.[9]

From the point of view of the UNV programme, the Volunteers are the key inputs that determine the outcomes of the activities of the programme. This was also recognized by the users and beneficiaries of the programme, who during the exploratory visits frequently mentioned the qualifications, experience, skills, and motivation of the Volunteers as factors determining the outcomes of the activities of the programme. These have, consequently, been included as explanatory variables in the conceptual framework. Other background variables that could conceivably influence the performance of the Volunteers, and which have been included in the framework, are the age, gender, nationality, and family situation of the Volunteers.

In their reports, the Volunteers themselves also identified a number of factors that affected their work, usually in a negative way. These included the rules, regulations, and procedures of the UN, which were considered too cumbersome by many of the Volunteers. Other issues that were identified and included in the framework as possible negative or positive influences are the remuneration, entitlements, conditions of service, status, and placement of the Volunteers.

A number of other issues, which were identified in previous studies, relate to the implementation of a project. These are the recruitment, orientation, briefings, training, and support provided to the Volunteers during their assignment, the length of the assignments, and the coordination with other international organizations. These have also been included in the framework as possible explanatory variables, in the category of variables that the UNV programme normally can influence.

Several other variables also relate to the design and implementation of a project, which in the past normally have been the responsibility of the UNDP, another UN agency, and the government ministry or institution where a UN Volunteer worked. From this category, variables that have been identified and included in the framework are the design of the project, the availability of co-workers, inputs and support from the government, work planning, management and supervision of the Volunteers, and coordination with government agencies and non-governmental organizations.[10]

Research related to World Bank projects shows that assistance to certain sectors has been more effective than assistance to other sectors in a number of countries. Although the projects where UN Volunteers have worked are usually very different from most World Bank programmes and projects, the sector in which a Volunteer worked was also included as an explanatory variable in the framework of the study.[11]

Finally, a number of contextual variables also exist that the UNV programme cannot influence, but that may affect the impact of the programme. Factors that have been identified and included in the framework are the national legislation, the administrative procedures of the government, the location of the assignment of the Volunteer, the climate, and the security situation, the economic situation, the social situation, the cultural situation, and the political situation in the country.[12]

A summary of the different variables identified that could influence the impact and perceived value of the UNV programme are shown in Figure 4.3 (page 54). In this framework, factors that the programme can influence and those that it has little or no control over have been separated for purposes of clarity.

Data collection and analysis

Questionnaires, which primarily contained close-ended questions, were developed and used in the study. Before the questionnaires were used, they were pre-tested, revised based on the pre-test, translated into Nepali, and field tested in Nepal. Different questionnaires were developed and used to collect data from former supervisors and co-workers of the UN Volunteers, beneficiaries of UNV assistance, the reference group, and the former Volunteers themselves.

All of the questionnaires included the main areas of focus of the study: human and social capital accumulation, changes in the availability of jobs, the level of poverty, women's lives, and the environment (objectives 1–3 of the study). Questions on factors that may

Figure 4.3 Conceptual framework for analysing the impact and perceived value of the UNV programme

Factors expected to influence outcomes

Volunteer characteristics[a]
qualifications, experience, skills, motivation, age, gender, nationality, and family situation of Volunteers

Terms and conditions[a]
rules, regulations, procedures, remuneration, entitlements conditions of service, status, and placement of Volunteers

Type of assignment[b]
sector, host, executing agency

External environment[b]
national legislation, administrative procedures, location, climate, security, economic, social, cultural, and political situation

(CONTEXT)

UNV contribution[a]
recruitment, orientation, briefings, training, support, determination of length and preparation of post description for the assignment

Counterpart contribution[b]
availability of and interaction with supervisors and co-workers, work planning, management, and supervision

Links and support[b]
link to and support from government agencies, international organizations, and non-governmental organizations

(INTERVENTION)

Outcomes

Impact of the programme
1. Human capital, measured through acquisition of new skills or knowledge.
2. Social capital, measured through changes in values and attitudes, motivation, cooperation, and participation.
3. Changes in job availability, poverty, women's lives, and the environment.

Perceived value of the programme
4. Relevance of the activities.
5. Performance of the Volunteers in comparison with other alternatives.
6. Sustainability, in terms of use of skills and knowledge, continuation of activities, and long-term benefits.

(RESULTS)

[a] Factors that can be influenced to a large extent by the head office of the UNV programme.
[b] Factors that can be influenced to a lesser extent – or not at all – by the head office of the UNV programme.

have affected the performance of the Volunteers and other aspects of the perceived value of the programme were included in the questionnaires to former Volunteers and respondents who had interacted significantly with the Volunteers (objectives 4–6 of the study).

Background information on how often the respondents had met with a Volunteer and how much time they had spent with the Volunteer was also included in the questionnaires. Information about the age, gender, and educational background of the respondents was also collected. For the Volunteers, the necessary background information about their age, gender, qualifications, experience, etc. could be obtained from the UNV head office and was therefore not included in the questionnaires.

At the time of the development of the questionnaires, a decision was made to use close-ended rather than open-ended questions. The reason was that it had been possible to identify the key issues and a range of answer options based on the reports reviewed and the exploratory visits. Open-ended questionnaires could have provided more in-depth information than close-ended questionnaires, but the responses would have been difficult to analyse for a large number of respondents. In the key area of human capital accumulation, however, respondents were able to list skills and knowledge that they had learned. The survey instruments also provided opportunities for the respondents to comment on other issues related to the UNV programme.[13]

In parallel with the development of the survey instruments, sampling and identification of respondents took place. All former Volunteers who had worked in Nepal during the period of the study and whose addresses could be retrieved were included in a mail survey. For the other respondents, however, a sample had to be drawn in order to keep the logistics of the study manageable. It was decided that limiting the number of interviews through sampling was preferable to reducing the number of different categories of respondents from whom information could be collected. The sampling of respondents for the interviews was done independently from the mail survey and was not influenced by the responses to the mail survey.

To select the interviewees for the study, a randomized, geographically stratified, and gender-balanced sample of 50 Volunteers was drawn. In addition, 15 replacements were identified. This was done in case it would not be possible to find supervisors, co-workers, or beneficiaries for some of the 50 Volunteers selected for the sample, or in case it would not be possible to complete the interviews for the sampled Volunteers for some other reason. In the end, 9 replacements had to be made.[14]

For each of the 50 Volunteers, 6 respondents were selected, which brought the total number of interviewees to 300. In most cases, only 1 supervisor and co-worker could be identified, so for these categories of respondents, the issue of selection of respondents did not arise. With regard to the beneficiaries and reference persons, there was usually a lot more choice and the surveyors were instructed to select 1 beneficiary and 2 reference persons who would be fairly representative of the community or organization where a particular Volunteer had worked. Although there was no deliberate strategy to ensure that the beneficiaries and reference group respondents were randomly selected, there is no reason to believe that any bias which would have distorted the findings of the study would have crept in.

Out of the total of 300 respondents identified, the results of 298 interviews could be used: 169 of these represented users and beneficiaries of the programme, that is, people who had professional contact with a particular Volunteer, while 129 of the respondents did not know a Volunteer whose work was assessed and therefore constituted the reference group. Where the final selection of respondents did not correspond to the underlying population of Volunteers, a correction was made by a weighting of responses.[15]

Structured interviews in Nepali or English were carried out with supervisors and co-workers of the 50 former Volunteers sampled for the survey, employees of government ministries and departments and international organizations, and members of non-governmental organizations and communities where the Volunteers had worked, that is, beneficiaries and reference group respondents.[16]

Additional information from the Volunteers whose work was

assessed was received through a mail survey. Of the 97 Volunteers who had served in Nepal during the period covered by the study, addresses of 85 could be located, and these Volunteers were included in the mail survey. The total number of responses to the survey, following a reminder sent to those who did not initially respond, was 48, that is, 56 per cent, which can be considered satisfactory. In the UNV community worker category the response rate was 50 per cent and in the UNV specialist category it was 63 per cent.

The data was coded and analysed using the Statistical Package for Social Sciences (SPSS).[17] The data analysis included one-way analyses of variance, and multiple linear and logistic regression analyses. The regression analyses were used to test if the interaction with Volunteers could explain differences in the responses of different respondents. Contact with Volunteers and four other explanatory variables were included in the analyses: the age, gender, and education of the respondents as well as the geographical location.[18]

Since the very beginning, the study faced two serious methodological constraints: the absence of any pre-intervention data, and the absence of a control group in the true sense of the word. A number of measures, therefore, had to be undertaken to strengthen the research design, to ensure the relevance and validity of the study, and to monitor the reliability and objectivity of the study continuously.[19]

Validity

From the outset, particular attention was given to ensure the internal validity of the study, that is, that the survey would capture and measure the main areas of focus of the study. Support for the validity of the conceptual model of the study was received through a factor analysis, which confirmed five of the seven key factors that had been identified in the conceptual framework of the study. The identified factors were: (i) the experience, competence, motivation, and origin of the Volunteers; (ii) the type of assignment of the Volunteers; (iii) the recruitment of the Volunteers; (iv) the link to and support from other organizations; and (v) the rules and conditions of the assignment. The two factors that did not stand out in the factor analysis were the external environment and the counterpart contribution.[20]

To enhance the validity of the survey instruments in terms of their content, comments on the draft questionnaires were requested and received from staff of the UNV programme and former Volunteers. Furthermore, in order to assess the face validity of the questionnaires, that is, how they would really work in practice, pilot tests were carried out in Nepal.[21]

The correlation between items in the questionnaires that measured similar things was calculated to assess the internal validity of the survey instruments. For instance, respondents who said that a Volunteer did a job that no one else locally could have done, should in most cases also have considered the performance of the UN Volunteer compared to a Nepalese national as good or very good. This indeed was the case, as is reflected in a significant correlation between these two items, which supports the internal validity of the questionnaires.[22]

In order to determine the construct validity of the study, the extent to which the questionnaires were able to discriminate between different categories of respondents was measured. This was done using a questionnaire item that assessed changes with respect to peace, democracy, and/or human rights. As expected, and as is explained below, the responses of the users and beneficiaries of the programme differed markedly from those of the reference group.

None of the Volunteers in Nepal had specifically worked on issues related to peace, democracy, or human rights, and it was therefore not expected that the Volunteers would have had much impact on these areas. At the same time, in view of the political changes that Nepal went through in the early 1990s, it was expected that the respondents in the reference group would indicate significant changes with regard to peace, democracy, and human rights in the country. This indeed was the case, which supports the argument that the items in the survey instruments were able to differentiate between different groups of respondents.[23]

To ensure the validity of the statistical conclusions of the study, methods for analysing the data were used in a standard way and results were interpreted carefully. To obtain more certainty regarding the relative magnitude of the changes that could be attributable to the work of the Volunteers, multiple regression analyses were complemented by logistic regression analyses, which are usually considered more robust under model misspecification.

To assess the external validity of the study, the methodology that was used in Nepal was also tested in Costa Rica and Mozambique. The questionnaires developed for Nepal were used in English in Costa Rica, translated into Portuguese for Mozambique, and administered with very good results in both countries. The fact that the survey instruments worked very well in very different contexts, and that the results from Mozambique and Costa Rica, albeit from a small number of respondents, were very much in line with the findings from Nepal, suggests a broader applicability of the methodology and supports the validity of the findings.

Reliability

To increase the reliability of the survey, two pilot tests of the questionnaires were conducted. Two different groups of respondents in different parts of Nepal were used in order to obtain as much feedback on the questionnaires as possible. Re-administering the questionnaires to the same group of respondents would have been a way to test if responses changed over time, but this was not considered necessary. The reason was that responses in the actual survey were expected to be stable, since the interviews in all but three cases were conducted more than a year after the Volunteers had left. Re-administering the questionnaires to the same respondents in the reference group could, however, have been useful since this might have uncovered some of the weaknesses with using a structured format for this category of respondents.

Although some difficulties with the structured format of the one-to-one interviews could be detected at the time of the pre-testing, it was still considered advantageous to collect data in a form where the results of the reference group interviews could be directly compared, item by item, with those of the supervisors, co-workers, and beneficiaries. An alternative, which was considered but rejected in favour of the structured interviews, was focus group discussions to learn about changes in the work environment of the UN Volunteers that had taken place without the involvement of the Volunteers.

Collecting information from a group of respondents against which to compare the assessments of the users and beneficiaries of the UNV programme was no doubt very good, but did pose some problems. The reference group consisted of employees of government departments and international organizations and members of communities who did not know a particular Volunteer. Since they could not be asked to assess the work of a Volunteer, they were asked more general questions about skills or knowledge they or other people in their community or organization had learned, changes in values and attitudes, the availability of jobs, poverty, women's lives, and the environment, etc. To several of the respondents these questions seemed somewhat vague or abstract, and the overall conclusion is that the survey instruments could have worked better in this group.

Another potential threat to the reliability of the study was the way the different respondents were selected. The reference group respondents, on the one hand, were selected specifically because they did not know a particular Volunteer; the users and beneficiaries of the programme, on the other hand, were chosen because they had professional contact with a particular Volunteer, and they knew this was the reason they were selected. If the selection procedure had an effect on the responses of the users and beneficiaries and not on the reference group, making comparisons between these two groups would have been problematic. This, however, does not seem to have been the case.

If indeed the responses of the users and beneficiaries, on the one hand, and the reference group, on the other hand, were different because of the way the respondents for the two groups were selected, one would have assumed differences between the two groups to be relatively consistent. However, once the respondents were divided into two groups based on their geographical location (Kathmandu and other areas of Nepal), a different pattern of responses emerged.

In Kathmandu, in terms of new skills or knowledge learned, for instance, there was not a significant difference between the users and beneficiaries, on the one hand, and the reference group, on the other hand. In areas outside Kathmandu the difference was significant. Among the users and beneficiaries, the difference between Kathmandu and other areas of Nepal was significant, while the difference in the reference group between Kathmandu and other areas of Nepal was almost significant.

Similar analyses relating to changes in social capital, jobs, poverty, women's lives, and the environment were also performed, with very similar results. Based on the results of these analyses, a proposition that the differences in the responses of the users and beneficiaries, on the one hand, and the reference group, on the other hand, would be a result of the way the respondents were selected must be rejected. This, thus, provides support for the overall reliability of the results of the study.

Another potential threat to the reliability of the survey could have been a tendency among respondents to select the middle option among the available answer options. In this study no such tendency could be detected while reviewing the responses to individual questionnaire items, which provides further support for the reliability of the survey.

The interviews were carried out by a total of 14 surveyors. It might seem that using a smaller number of surveyors would have been better in order to ensure consistency in the way the information was collected. It was, however, considered that the advantages of using a rather large number of surveyors did outweigh any potential loss in terms of accuracy or consistency in the way the interviews were conducted. Particular emphasis was given to the training of the surveyors to ensure that they all knew exactly what to do and what was expected from them. In the end, the performance of the surveyors was very good, and the results of all but 2 out of 300 interviews completed could be used.

Using a smaller number of surveyors would have increased the time needed to complete the survey considerably. Including travel time, the 14 surveyors needed 221 days in all to complete the 300 interviews, which corresponds to 37 weeks, or more than 9 months, of work for one person using a six day working week. The average number of interviews completed by individual surveyors was 21, and ranged from 49 in the capital Kathmandu to 12 in the least accessible parts of western Nepal. The number of surveyors could have been reduced somewhat, but the capacity and availability of the surveyors also partly determined their number. Other factors and practical considerations that also drove the data collection included cost and weather. The data collection was timed to take place during the winter months when the weather would be pleasant and travelling would not be made difficult by monsoon rains.

Of the 97 Volunteers who had served in Nepal between 1987 and 1996, 85 Volunteers whose addresses could be located were included in the mail survey. Responses were requested within 5 weeks from the date the questionnaires were mailed. A total of 42 responses (49 per cent) were received within 2 months from the time the questionnaires were mailed. At this time a reminder, along with a copy of the questionnaire, was re-sent to all Volunteers who had not responded. This resulted in 6 additional responses, bringing the total number of responses to 48 (56 per cent).

While 56 per cent of the Volunteers did respond to the survey, it is still possible that these respondents are not entirely representative of the Volunteers who served in Nepal during 1987–96. Of the Volunteers who responded, most seemed to have had a positive experience. Not all, however, had a positive experience, and of the four Volunteers included in the sample whose contracts were prematurely terminated, two responded to the mail survey. This may be seen as an argument against any bias in the findings that could have resulted if only the views of the Volunteers who had a positive experience were included in the findings of the study.

Objectivity and relevance

One reason for recruiting and training a group of local surveyors was to be able to complete the data collection in as short a period as possible. Another reason was to try to ensure the neutrality and lack of bias of the survey. It was thought that using surveyors from Nepal, who spoke the local language and who were not associated with the UNV programme in any way, would be able to obtain more frank and honest responses than one or several external interviewers who in one way or another would have been perceived as linked to the UNV programme.

Another way to try to minimize any bias and increase confidence in the findings of the study was to use data from as many different sources as possible. These included previous studies, reports prepared by Volunteers, interviews with users and beneficiaries of the pro- gramme, external referees, and a mail survey to former Volunteers.[24]

Although some of the respondents who were interviewed indicated that certain items in the questionnaires were not applicable or rele- vant to them, the research questions and focus of the study remained relevant throughout the evaluation. While the study focuses on one country, it provides insights that should be relevant to the UNV programme as a whole. The results of the study and the lessons learned are also expected to be of interest and relevance to the UNDP and other funds, programmes, and agencies of the UN system as well as a more general audience interested in the work of the UN.

Notes

1. For a presentation of content analysis as a method, see: Krippendorff, Klaus. *Content Analysis: An Introduction to Its Methodology.* Thousand Oaks, CA: Sage, 1980.
2. 11 Volunteers completed two assignments in Nepal, and one Volunteer completed three assignments during the period covered by the study. Even if the number of Volunteers who served in Nepal (97) is used to calculate the percentage of end-of-assignment reports available, 61 per cent is still a low response rate on which to base any analysis of the outcomes of the work of the volunteers.

3. For a more detailed discussion on meta-analysis as an approach, see: Valadez, Joseph and Michael Bamberger, eds. *Monitoring and Evaluating Social Programmes in Developing Countries*, EDI Development Studies. Washington, DC: The World Bank, 1994, pp. 64–65.

4. A similar conclusion can be found in a study commissioned by the Development Assistance Committee of the OECD, which tries to synthesize evaluations on the impact of development projects and programmes of non-governmental organizations. This report raises serious questions about the quality of the evaluation reports, which constitute the basis for the synthesis study. See: Riddell, Roger C. and others. *Searching for Impact and Methods: NGO Evaluation Synthesis Study*, Ministry for Foreign Affairs of Finland, Department for International Development Cooperation, Report 1997:2. Helsinki: Hakapaino, 1998, pp. 11–13.

5. Through discussions with members of communities, organizations, and government departments where Volunteers had worked, the research design and the conceptual framework of the study were developed further. For a discussion on the benefits of exploratory work as part of the development of survey, see: Valadez, Joseph and Michael Bamberger, eds. *Monitoring and Evaluating Social Programmes in Developing Countries*, EDI Development Studies. Washington, DC: The World Bank, 1994, pp. 296–297.

6. Carvalho, Soniya and Howard White discuss the different emphases of different disciplines in the assessment of programmes and projects in *Implementing Projects for the Poor: What Has Been Learned?* Directions in Development. Washington, DC: World Bank, 1996, pp. 5–8.

7. United Nations Volunteers. "The Appropriate Use of Volunteers in Development". *United Nations Volunteers Thematic Series*, Programme Advisory Note. Geneva: UNV, 1991.

8. Logical frameworks, often referred to as a "LogFrames", have been a tool used for many years, in various adaptations, by the UN organizations and other agencies, for planning, managing, and evaluating development projects. For an overview of different logical frameworks, see: MacArthur, John D. "Logical Frameworks Today – Increased Diversification of the Planning Format". In: Kirkpatrick, Colin and Jon Weiss, eds. *Cost-benefit Analysis and Project Appraisal in Developing Countries*. Brookfield, VT: Edward Elgar, 1996, pp. 128–143.

9. For a sample of the logical framework that has been used by the UNDP and several other UN agencies, see: United Nations Development Programme. *How to Write a Project Document*. New York: UNDP, 1990, pp. 2–8.

10. A description of how political considerations, rather than the priorities of local people, affect the allocation of resources can be found in Blakie, Piers, John Cameron, and David Seddon. *Nepal in Crises: Growth and Stagnation at the Periphery*. Oxford: Clarendon Press, 1980.

11. Carvalho, Soniya and Howard White. *Implementing Projects for the Poor: What Has Been Learned?* Directions in Development. Washington, DC: World Bank, 1996, p. 6. See also Israel, Arturo. *Institutional Development: Incentives to Performance*. Baltimore: Johns Hopkins Press, 1987, for a discussion on differences in specification of benefits and competition as explanations as to why World Bank assistance to certain sectors such as industry, telecommunications, and utilities

may have been more effective than assistance to other sectors, such as education and services.

12. For a discussion on the importance of the social and cultural context for the effectiveness of development projects, see: Cernea, Michael, ed. *Putting People First: Sociological Variables in Rural Development*, 2nd edn. New York: Oxford University Press, 1991.

13. At the time of the design of the survey instruments it became evident that some of the questions would not be relevant to all Volunteer assignments, e.g., those of a primarily administrative nature. It was, however, considered better not to exclude certain categories of Volunteers in order not to manipulate the sample, and to have uniform survey instruments for all respondents so as to be able to compare the responses of all respondents. This was considered important in order to be able to present a more accurate picture of the impact of the UNV programme in Nepal – including assignments that may have had little or no impact because a Volunteer had done little else except administered fellow Volunteers, a UN programme, or an office. During the actual interviews, how-ever, only a few of the respondents indicated to the surveyors that some of the questions were not relevant to their situation.

14. In a country such as Nepal, which is characterized by a difficult terrain and poor communications to many parts of the country, the geographical location of the assignments of the Volunteers was considered important. Therefore, the sample was divided over the five administrative regions of Nepal, the Eastern, Central, Western, Mid-Western, and Far-Western regions, and the capital city of Kathmandu. The next criteria that was used in the sampling was gender balance. The original balance between male and female Volunteers in the two sub-populations (approximately 3:2 for UNV specialists, and 4:1 for UNV community workers) was to remain in the sample. Finally, it was decided that an individual Volunteer should appear only once in the sample even if he or she had completed more than one assignment and could technically have been in-cluded a second time in a randomized, geographically stratified, and gender-balanced sample.

15. In order to prevent any estimation bias that could have resulted from the replacements that had to be made during the course of the study, a weighting of responses was introduced at the time of the analysis of the data. The correction that had to be made was needed to address the over-representation of female Volunteers and the under-representation of male Volunteers in the sample. Weights in the form

$$w_q = 1/q$$

were introduced to make the necessary corrections. In these expressions q equals the number of (either male or female) Volunteers sampled over the number of Volunteers who should have been sampled from the two sub-populations of UNV specialists and UNV community workers. For instance, out of the total 25 community workers who were sampled, 17 were males. The correct number would have been 20, therefore, $q = 17/20$ and $w_q = 1.18$. This means that the responses of each of the 17 male community workers have been weighted up by a factor of 1.18, thus producing a combined result that is equivalent to that of 20 unweighted responses of male community workers, which is correct.

16. As was expected, some respondents, particularly those who worked in government ministries and UN agencies in Kathmandu, felt somewhat constrained by the structured format of the questionnaires and perceived that they could not enter into a dialogue with the surveyors. Because of the way the study was designed, however, it was never intended to encourage dialogue between surveyors and respondents, and it was in fact anticipated that some respondents would feel somewhat frustrated by the structured format. The advantages and disadvantages of the methodology chosen, and the questionnaires used, had, however, been weighed against using semi-structured interviews or another similar approach that would have required setting up the research differently in terms of the number, qualifications, and experience of the surveyors as well as the training and supervision provided to them.

17. For one of the outcome variables, changes in human capital, interval level data were obtained and used. For the other outcome variables, ordinal level data were obtained and used once responses had been coded from five-point scales such as: "very negative", "negative", "none", "positive", and "very positive". In addition, arithmetic averages of four ordinal level questions were used as indicators of specific outcomes: changes in social capital or changes in UNDP's priority areas. For a discussion of potential problems with using a summation of ordinal level data to create an index, such as the one used to measure social capital development, see: Valadez, Joseph and Michael Bamberger, eds. *Monitoring and Evaluating Social Programs in Developing Countries*, EDI Development Studies. Washington, DC: The World Bank, 1994, p. 202.

18. Human capital was measured using the number of skills learned and areas of new knowledge acquired that the respondents indicated. Social capital was measured using an unweighted average of the responses to four questions that assessed changes in (i) values and attitudes, (ii) motivation, (iii) cooperation, and (iv) participation of people in local affairs; in addition, the individual components of social capital were examined. Changes with respect to UNDP's priority areas were analysed using an unweighted average of the responses to four questions dealing with changes in (i) job availability, (ii) poverty, (iii) women's lives, and (iv) the environment, as well as through an analysis of the responses to the four individual questionnaire items. The other outcome variables related to the performance of the Volunteers and the relevance, results, and sustainability of the activities of the Volunteers were measured using individual items from the questionnaires. The explanatory variables (see Fig. 4.3) included quantitative variables (e.g., age of the respondents), qualitative variables with multiple categories (e.g., very poor, poor, OK, good, very good), as well as variables with only two values or levels (e.g., gender, or contact with the Volunteers). To facilitate the analysis, qualitative variables with multiple categories were where possible recoded as "dummy variables", i.e., with only two values. In the case of geographical location, for instance, the two values used were the capital city and other parts of Nepal.

19. See: Caudle, Sharon L. "Using Qualitative Approaches". In: Wholey,

Joseph S., Harry P. Hatry, and Kathryn E. Newcomer, eds. *Handbook of Practical Program Evaluation*. San Francisco: Jossey-Bass, 1994, pp. 84–93.

20. The total number of issues identified that could influence the work of the Volunteers for which data could be obtained was 64 (see Fig. 4.3). To determine which individual items to include in the factor analysis, bivariate correlation coefficients between the individual explanatory variables and the outcome variables (changes in human capital, changes in social capital, and changes in the UNDP's priority areas) were calculated. All items which had a significant correlation ($p < 0.05$) with one of the outcome variables were included in the factor analysis. This reduced the number of explanatory variables from 64 to 28. Following an exploratory factor analysis to identify principal components of the 28 explanatory variables, a varimax rotation was performed using unweighted least squares. This resulted in eight interpretable factors, five of which corresponded to the seven key factors identified in the conceptual model of the study.

21. Cook, Thomas H. and Donald T. Campbell. *Quasi Experimentation: Design and Analysis Issues for Field Setting*. Boston: Houghton-Mifflin, 1979, break down the concept of validity into four components: internal validity, construct validity, statistical conclusion validity, and external validity.

22. The correlation between the two items that tested the internal validity of the questionnaire was statistically significant ($r = 0.35$, $p < 0.01$).

23. Throughout this chapter, a significant difference refers to a probability of a difference of more than 95 per cent ($p < 0.05$). For an overview of recent economic, political, and social changes in Nepal, see, e.g., Karan, Pradyumna P. and Hiroshi Ishii. *Nepal: A Himalayan Kingdom in Transition*. Tokyo: The United Nations University Press, 1996.

24. For a discussion on the systematic use and comparison of independent data collection methods, known as "triangulation", see, e.g., Valadez, Joseph and Michael Bamberger, eds. *Monitoring and Evaluating Social Programmes in Developing Countries*, EDI Development Studies. Washington, DC: The World Bank, 1994, pp. 224–225.

5

Findings

Impact of the programme

The impact of the UNV programme was determined based on an assessment of the extent to which the programme was able to achieve its objectives and fulfil its two main mandates – strengthening human and social capital in developing countries. In addition, the impact on the UNDP's four broad priority areas during the 10 years covered by the study was evaluated. This included an assessment of changes in the availability of jobs, the level of poverty, women's lives, and the environment. A summary of the findings relating to the impact of the programme are presented below, with more details given in Appendix A.

Changes in human capital

To assess changes in human capital, respondents were asked to list new skills or knowledge that they, or others in their communities or workplace, had learned. According to 9 out of 10 of the users and beneficiaries of the programme (90.3 per cent), the Volunteers had been able to transfer skills or knowledge as part of their assignment. The average number of skills, or areas in which new knowledge had been transferred by the Volunteers, was 2.8. Areas or fields in which transfer of skills and knowledge by the Volunteers took place included planning, administration, information, communication, education, vocational training, family planning, health, nutrition, agriculture, animal husbandry, forestry, fisheries, handicrafts, income generation, and community development.

Specific skills transferred by the Volunteers included, among others, project management, production of audio-visual materials, preparation of maps, computer programming, plumbing, car mechanics, garment making, curriculum development, development of teaching methods and materials, literacy for adults, preventive health care, personal hygiene, sanitation, disease control, vegetable growing, animal raising, poultry farming, fish farming, bee keeping, and jewellry making.

Based on not only the number of skills or the new knowledge transferred by the Volunteers, but also on the variety of different areas that the skills and knowledge represent, the Volunteers can be said to have had a positive impact on human capital in Nepal during the period covered by the study. This is notwithstanding the short-coming of the number of new skills and new areas of knowledge as an indicator of human capital. It is, in addition, also important to note that other people in the communities and organizations where the Volunteers worked, but who did not have any contact with the Volunteers, also acquired a considerable amount of skills and knowledge, albeit in many cases in somewhat different areas than the users and beneficiaries of the UNV programme.

If a major change in human capital is understood as the acquisition of three or more skills, or new knowledge in three or more areas, there was a significant difference between the users and beneficiaries of the programme, on the one hand, and the reference group, on the other hand. Results of a logistic regression analysis showed that those who had contact with the Volunteers indicated significantly greater positive changes in human capital. The odds of a major positive change in human capital were 1.8 times greater among the users and beneficiaries of the programme than in the reference group. The odds, however, depended on how a major and minor change in human capital were defined. This needs to be kept in mind when presenting an overall positive conclusion of the impact of the UNV programme on human capital.[1]

The biggest impact of the programme on human capital could be found in areas outside the capital city, Kathmandu, where the amount of skills and knowledge acquired by the users and beneficiaries was significantly greater than in the reference group. The users and beneficiaries of the programme also indicated that Volunteers in areas outside Kathmandu had transferred significantly more skills and knowledge than the Volunteers in Kathmandu. This could be because people in areas outside Kathmandu started from a lower level of skills and knowledge, or because the assignments of the Volunteers in Kathmandu were very different from those of the Volunteers outside the capital. This, however, does not change the basic finding of the study that the programme in terms of human capital development had its greatest impact in areas outside the capital city.

Changes in social capital

The second objective of the study focused on changes in social capital in communities or organizations where UN Volunteers had worked. The components of social capital that were measured included people's values and attitudes, motivation, cooperation, and participation in local affairs.

In terms of social capital, the Volunteers also appear to have had a positive impact. Four out of five of the respondents (ranging from 77.9 to 83.3 per cent) considered that the Volunteers had a positive or very positive effect on the values and attitudes, motivation, cooperation, and participation of people in the community or organization where a Volunteer had worked. Meanwhile, one in every five or six of the respondents (between 16.7 and 22.1 per cent) did not think the Volunteers had a positive effect on people's values and attitudes, motivation, cooperation, or participation in local affairs.

Respondents who had contact with the Volunteers reported a significantly larger positive change in social capital overall, measured as an unweighted average of the four components of social capital used in this study: change in people's values and attitudes, motivation, cooperation, and participation in local affairs. The biggest differences between the users and beneficiaries of the programme, on the one hand, and the reference group, on the other hand, could be found in areas outside Kathmandu. The programme thus appears to have been most successful in terms of social capital development in areas outside the capital city.

Using multiple regression analyses, statistically significant differences in favour of the users and beneficiaries of the programme could be found with respect to three components of social capital: people's motivation, cooperation, and participation in local affairs. The results of logistic regression analyses were not statistically significant, but respondents who had contact with the Volunteers were 2.11 times more likely to indicate a positive change in people's participation in local affairs than those who had no contact with the Volunteers. The odds for a positive change were 1.65 times higher in the case of people's motivation among the respondents who had contact with the Volunteers compared to respondents who had no contact with the Volunteers. In the case of people's cooperation, the corresponding odds were 1.30 times higher, and in the case of people's values and attitudes 1.17 times higher.

Changes in jobs, poverty, women's lives, and the environment

To measure other outcomes of the work of the Volunteers, in addition to human and social capital formation, the effect of the Volunteers was assessed on the priority areas of the UNDP: job creation, poverty reduction, environmental protection, and advancement of women.

A large majority (between 55.9 and 66.9 per cent) considered the effect of the Volunteers on these four priority areas of the UNDP, jobs, poverty, environment, and women, to be positive or very positive. Approximately one-third of the respondents (between 32.5 and 42.9 per cent) did not think the Volunteers had any effect on the availability of jobs, the level of poverty, women's lives, or the environment. Only one or two respondents (0.6 or 1.2 per cent), however, thought the Volunteers had a negative or very negative effect on any one of the UNDP's four priority areas.

Positive changes relating to the availability of jobs, the level of poverty, and the environment that were attributed to the work of the Volunteers by the users and beneficiaries of the programme were significantly greater than the corresponding changes indicated by the reference group. Both multiple regression analyses and logistic regression analyses yielded the same results. The odds of a positive change among the users and beneficiaries were 1.58 times higher with respect to the availability of jobs, 2.25 times higher with respect to the level of poverty, and 2.28 times higher with respect to the environment, compared to the reference group. Users and beneficiaries in areas outside Kathmandu indicated significantly greater positive changes with respect to jobs, poverty, and the environment than the users and beneficiaries in Kathmandu.

In terms of changes in women's lives, on the other hand, those indicated by the respondents in the reference group were more positive than the changes in women's lives that were attributed to the work of the Volunteers, although the difference was not statistically significant, except in the capital Kathmandu. This is consistent with the finding that the programme appears to have had its biggest positive impact on the other three priority areas of the UNDP, jobs, poverty, and the environment, in locations outside the capital.

Perceived value of the programme

The assessment of the perceived value of the UNV programme was based on the following criteria: the relevance of the activities of the Volunteers, the performance of the Volunteers in comparison to other available alternatives, and the results of the activities of the Volunteers and their sustainability. A summary of the findings is given below. Additional details are given in Appendix B.

Overall, very few users and beneficiaries (between 3.0 and 10.8 per cent) gave a negative rating (very poor or poor) to any of the items that were used to determine the perceived value of the programme. Although the middle option (OK) was selected by at least one in four respondents (between 24.9 and 42.0 per cent), a majority of the respondents (between 51.8 and 72.1 per cent) gave a positive rating (good or very good) to the different items that assessed the perceived value of the programme. In other words, there was a clear tilting of the responses towards the positive ratings.

In terms of negative responses, the largest number of the respondents (10.8 per cent) considered the continuation of the activities started by the Volunteers as very poor or poor. The long-term benefits of the activities of the Volunteers, a second aspect of sustainability, also had a comparable number of responses marked very poor or poor (8.4 per cent). A significant number (15.2 per cent) of the respondents also indicated no or very little use of skills or knowledge learned, which was the third aspect of sustainability measured.

Relevance

An overall assessment that can be made is that the programme was considered relevant to the needs of the country during the period covered by the study. This can be said based on the fact that almost two-thirds of the respondents (65.9 per cent) rated the relevance of the work of the Volunteers as good or very good, and more than half of them (54.1 per cent) indicated that the Volunteers did a job that no one else locally could have done. The work of the Volunteers was considered most relevant in areas outside Kathmandu, where UNV community workers were particularly perceived to have done a job that no one else locally could have done.

Performance of the Volunteers

In terms of the performance of the Volunteers, the programme scored well: three out of five (61.0 per cent) rated the effectiveness of the Volunteers as good or very good. More than two-thirds (69.5 per cent) thought the performance of the UN Volunteers in comparison to other volunteers was good or very good.

When compared to international experts, more than half of the respondents (53.2 per cent) considered the performance of the Volunteers to be good or very good, and a very small number (8.9 per cent) indicated that the performance was poor or very poor. This is an interesting finding considering that the average cost of an international expert is normally at least three or four times that of a UN Volunteer.

More than two-thirds of the respondents (69.8 per cent) considered the performance of the Volunteers good or very good in comparison to the performance of other non-Nepalese nationals, such as expatriates on direct contract with the Nepalese Government, seconded, or on loan from another government.

Approximately half of the respondents (53.1 per cent) considered the performance of the Volunteers good or very good compared to the performance of Nepalese nationals. A rather large number of respondents (42.0 per cent) rated the performance of the Volunteers in comparison to a Nepalese national as OK. In this context it may also be worth noting that almost half (45.9 per cent) of the respondents had indicated that the Volunteers did a job that someone else locally could have done. What these findings seem to imply is that even if the overall performance of the Volunteers was considered good, the work of the Volunteers may in many cases not have been indispensable. This seems to have been the case particularly in the capital, Kathmandu.

Of the different questions that assessed the performance of the Volunteers, the only one where there was a significant difference in the rating of the UNV specialists and the UNV community workers was the one that compared the Volunteers to Nepalese nationals. In comparison to Nepalese nationals, the rating of the UNV community workers who had worked in Kathmandu was significantly more favourable than the rating of the UNV specialists who had worked in Kathmandu.

Results and sustainability

In terms of the results of the programme, almost three out of four respondents (72.1 per cent) considered these good or very good. This was true for UNV specialists and even more so for UNV community workers. Also, despite dissatisfaction by a small number of users and beneficiaries (8.4 per cent) with the long-term benefits of the activities of the Volunteers, a large majority of the respondents (63.5 per cent) considered these good or very good.

The overall performance of the programme in terms of the sustainability of the results can, however, not be considered entirely satisfactory given that only half of the respondents (51.8 per cent) considered the continuation of the activities started by the Volunteers good or very good, and taking into account that a significant number of respondents thought the continuation of the activities was poor or very poor (10.8 per cent). Moreover, less than half of the respondents (40.0 per cent) indicated that they or others in their community or organization had used skills or knowledge taught by the Volunteers a lot or very much. In the reference group, the mean use of skills and knowledge was somewhat higher than among the users and beneficiaries, but the difference was not statistically significant.

Other findings

In this section, the role of the head office of the UNV programme is reviewed, and the effect of external factors on the work of the Volunteers are summarized. Since data were collected from Volunteers as well as their former supervisors, co-workers, and beneficiaries, it was also possible to compare the assessments of the Volunteers of their work and performance with those of the users and beneficiaries of the programme. These results are also presented below, along with the views of the Volunteers of the perceived value of the programme to themselves. More details of the other findings of the study are given in Appendix B.

The role of UNV headquarters

A number of functions that the UNV headquarters perform were identified as critical in previous evaluations, or during the exploratory visits, and therefore are included in the study. Both previous evaluation reports and many of the users and the Volunteers interviewed during the exploratory visits were critical of the headquarters of the UNV programme with respect to a number of issues. Based on this study, however, the headquarters of the programme can be rather satisfied with its performance in the past.

Most of the users gave good marks to the UNV head office for the way in which it carried out its primary functions: the identification of Volunteers, matching of Volunteers with posts, and arranging for their recruitment. Three-quarters (75.0 and 74.5 per cent, respectively) considered the competence and motivation of the Volunteers good or very good, and approximately two-thirds (64.6 and 60.4 per cent, respectively) thought the matching of the Volunteers with posts and the recruitment process were good or very good. Among the Volunteers themselves, three-quarters (79.2 and 75.0 per cent, respectively) considered the matching and the recruitment process good or very good.

Responsibilities of the head office of the UNV programme also include ensuring that the host organization where a Volunteer works is adequately briefed, and that appropriate language and other training is provided to a Volunteer. Although there seems to be scope for improvement in the these areas, particularly with regard to the language training, a large majority ·of the users (between 58.2 and 78.0 per cent) and Volunteers (between 68.9 and 74.4 per cent) considered that the effect of the briefing of the host organizations, and the language and other training, was positive or very positive.

The length of the assignment of the Volunteers, which in most cases was 2 years, was considered too short by nearly half of the Volunteers and half of the users. Approximately two in five of the users (41.2 per cent) and almost one in five of the Volunteers (16.7

per cent) perceived that this had a negative effect on the work of the Volunteers.

Findings from previous studies, which this study was able to confirm, were that the availability of co-workers, and to a lesser extent the management and supervision of the Volunteers, were considered problematic by a number of Volunteers (22.7 per cent and 14.6 per cent, respectively). These are issues, however, which the headquarters of the UNV programme has rather limited ways of influencing. Something that may be even more important than the availability of co-workers, which may have been overlooked in the past, is the (lack of) teaching or training experience of the Volunteers. The background data on the Volunteers indicated that none of them had any previous teaching or training experience. Four out of five had said that they did not have any experience and the rest did not respond to the question.

Of the Volunteers, one in five (19.2 per cent) of the UNV specialists and almost three-quarters (72.7 per cent) of the UNV community workers expressed dissatisfaction with their monthly living allowance. Almost half of the UNV community workers (44.4 per cent) thought that their living allowance had a negative or very negative effect on their work.

Although, based on the results of this survey, the overall assessment of the headquarters of the UNV programme is positive, there is no room for complacency. The study covers the period from 1987 to 1996, which means that the results pertaining to the identification, recruitment, and training of the Volunteers relate to a period before and up to 1994. It is therefore possible that the performance of the head office deteriorated in the early 1990s, at a time when the programme grew considerably and began funding projects of its own, which would explain the dissatisfaction expressed by a number of users and Volunteers during the exploratory visits in late 1995 and early 1996.

Another possible explanation of the difference in the views expressed by the current users and current Volunteers, and those of past users and past Volunteers, at least as far as the recruitment of a Volunteer is concerned, is that the delays in the fielding of a Volunteer, for instance, may seem very important at the time a Volunteer arrives, but may in retrospect not really have affected the work or performance of a Volunteer very much.

Many of the comments provided by the interviewees stressed the importance of the language abilities of the Volunteers. The fact that language training did not emerge as an even more important issue in the statistical analyses of the questionnaire items may be explained by the fact that the particular questionnaire item appears to blur the distinction between the language training activity and the language ability of the Volunteers.

What was learned during the exploratory visits was that many of the Volunteers who perceived a real need to learn the local language did so on their own without waiting for training to be provided by the head office of the UNV programme; thus, in hindsight, the language training was really not an issue to many respondents, since the Volunteers demonstrated the required language ability.

Effects of the external environment

The study also looked at a number of factors that may have affected the work of the Volunteers, even if these were considered largely beyond the control of the UNV headquarters, such as links between the activities of the Volunteers and those of other organizations as well as support for the activities of the Volunteers. As could be expected, the effect of the links to other organizations and support was considered positive by most users of the programme and, even more so, by the Volunteers.

Four out of five of the users (between 80.9 and 88.2 per cent) and the Volunteers (between 84.1 and 91.3 per cent) considered the effect of links to other government agencies, international organizations, or non-governmental organizations positive. Financial support was mainly provided by the UN, and considered positive by more than three-quarters of the users and Volunteers (80.4 per cent, for both categories). A vast majority of the Volunteers (between 72.1

and 89.7 per cent) also considered support other than financial assistance from the government, the UN, or other international organizations as positive.

A very large majority (between 73.1 and 89.9 per cent) of the users did not perceive that the external factors, such as the climate, or the social, cultural, economic, political, or security situation, had any effect on the work of the Volunteers. Among the Volunteers themselves, the number of respondents who felt the external environment had no effect was somewhat smaller (between 55.3 and 83.3 per cent), and the number of respondents who perceived the effect was negative was correspondingly bigger. Of the external factors, the effect of the political and economic situation was considered negative by the largest number of Volunteers (40.4 and 34.9 per cent, respectively).

A small number of users (between 11.4 and 17.3 per cent) thought the rules and procedures of the UNV programme, the government, or the UN had a negative effect on the work of the Volunteers. Among the Volunteers, one in five (20.5 per cent) considered that the rules and procedures of the government had a negative effect on their work, but only two respondents (4.4 per cent) said this about the rules and procedures of the UN and UNV. More than one in every four of the Volunteers thought the effect of the UN and UNV rules and procedures on their work was positive (26.7 and 31.9 per cent, respectively).

Self-evaluation

The study also provided an opportunity to compare the responses of the Volunteers to those of their former supervisors, co-workers, and the beneficiaries of their work. As could be expected, the Volunteers' estimates of their achievements and the perceived value of their work were, in general, higher than those of the users and beneficiaries of the programme. This was particularly true for the UNV specialists, who estimated their achievements and the value of their work on average 1.70 times higher than their former supervisors, co-workers, and beneficiaries. The biggest differences in the assessments related to perceptions of the influence of the Volunteers on peace, democracy and/or human rights, women's lives, and perceptions of the Volunteers having performed a job which no one else locally could have done.

The assessments of the UNV community workers and those of the users and beneficiaries of the programme came quite close on many issues, and on a few issues, the UNV community workers even underestimated their achievements and performance compared to the assessments of the users and beneficiaries. On average, however, the UNV community workers' estimates of their achievements and the value of their work were 1.12 times higher than those of their former supervisors, co-workers, and beneficiaries. On two issues, the continuation of the activities started by the Volunteers and their long-term benefits, the assessments of the UNV community workers were much more positive than those of the users and beneficiaries of the programme.

Based on this survey, the benefits of the programme to the Volunteers appear very big. Four out of five of the Volunteers considered that they had learned a lot or very much in terms of new skills and knowledge, and increased their understanding of another culture by a lot or very much (79.2 and 87.5 per cent, respectively). The benefits of working as a UN Volunteer for another job were, however, only considered important by one-third of the Volunteers (32.6 per cent). The views of the UNV specialists and UNV community workers were very similar, and the assessments of the users of the programmes of the benefits to the Volunteers corresponded very well with those of the Volunteers, although the users' assessments of the benefits to the Volunteers were overall more reserved. All in all, the results pertaining to the perceived value of the programme to the Volunteers underline what could be referred to as the two-way nature of the programme, that is, that the Volunteers as part of their assignments both give and receive.

Note

1. Throughout the presentation of the findings of this study, a significant difference refers to a probability of a difference of more than 95 per cent ($p < 0.05$).

6

Conclusions

The primary purpose of this study was to assess the UNV programme in terms of its impact. The impact of the programme was determined based on an assessment of the achievement of the objectives of the programme. In addition, the study assessed the value of the programme as perceived by the users and beneficiaries of the programme. One country, Nepal, was used as a case study for the assessment. The study covered the period from 1987 to 1996.

In trying to determine whether the programme had any impact and how the users and beneficiaries perceived the value of the programme, the study addressed six different issues. The first three of these measured the impact of the programme, the latter three determined the perceived value of the programme:

1. changes in human capital
2. changes in social capital
3. changes in job opportunities, poverty, women's lives, and the environment
4. the relevance of the work of the Volunteers
5. the performance of the Volunteers
6. the results and sustainability of the work of the Volunteers.

The broader purpose of the evaluation of the UNV programme was to serve as a case study of the impact of development cooperation activities of the UN, understood as the extent to which a UN programme achieves its objectives and produces desired outcomes. Finally, the study also attempted to demonstrate a methodology that could be used to assess the impact of other UN funds, programmes, and specialized agencies.

Summary of findings

The first general conclusion of the study is that the UNV programme appears to have had an impact on the communities and organizations in Nepal where the UN Volunteers worked during the period covered by the study. A positive impact of the programme could be found on human and social capital accumulation and with respect to changes in the environment, the level of poverty, and the availability of jobs; with respect to changes in women's lives, a positive impact was less evident. Overall, the impact of the programme was most notable in areas outside the capital Kathmandu.

The programme was rated very highly by the users and beneficiaries of the programme with regard to its relevance and the performance of the Volunteers. In terms of the sustainability of the activities initiated by the programme, more could still be done to ensure lasting benefits of the programme. Both the users of the programme and the Volunteers themselves appreciated the performance of the head office of the UNV programme, and the Volunteers indicated that they had benefited considerably from participating in the programme.

Although too many or too far-reaching conclusions regarding the impact of the UNV programme in other countries should not be drawn based on this one case study, the findings of the study should be relevant to the programme as a whole. One reason for this is that the UNV programme in Nepal during the period covered by the study was both representative and typical of the UNV programme as a whole, in terms of the variety of Volunteer assignments and sectors of work, profiles, and experience of the Volunteers, male to female ratios, etc.

A second reason to consider the findings as relevant to the programme as a whole is that the methodology used in Nepal was also tested in Africa (Mozambique) and Latin America (Costa Rica), with very similar results as in Nepal. Even if the number of interviews completed in Mozambique and Costa Rica were much smaller than in Nepal, the questionnaires worked equally well in African, Latin American, and Asian contexts and the views of the users and beneficiaries concerning the impact of the programme were very similar on all three continents. These results, along with the results of other analyses performed, support the validity and reliability of the findings of the study.

Impact of the programme

In a relative sense, the programme had the biggest positive impact on human and social capital development as well as on changes with respect to the environment, the level of poverty, and the availability of jobs, which represent three of the UNDP's four priority areas in the late 1980s and the first half of the 1990s. The programme also had a positive impact on women's lives, but the relative importance of the programme in this area appeared smaller. The impact of the programme was particularly noticeable in areas outside the capital Kathmandu.

When compared to definitions of human capital by Gary Becker and others, which include areas such as the health of people, the indicator of human capital used in this study, the number of skills or new knowledge acquired from the Volunteers, must be considered rather narrow. Despite this, the UNV programme can be said to have had an impact on human capital in Nepal.

Nine out of ten of the users and beneficiaries of the programme indicated that the Volunteers had transferred skills or knowledge as part of their assignment. Most users and beneficiaries indicated three as the number of skills transferred by, or areas in which knowledge was acquired from, the Volunteers. The odds of a major change in human capital, defined as three or more skills acquired, or acquisition of new knowledge in three or more areas, was 1.80 times greater among the users and beneficiaries of the programme than in the reference group.

The relative importance of the impact of the UNV programme must, however, be considered contingent upon how human capital is defined and how a change in human capital is measured. A significant amount of learning also took place in communities and organizations during the period covered by this study without any influence of the UNV programme, through other programmes and no doubt the media as well. The biggest positive impact of the programme on human capital could be found in smaller towns and rural areas.

The impact of the programme on social capital also appears very positive. More than four out of five respondents thought the Volunteers had a positive or very positive effect on the motivation and co-operation of people in their community or the organization where they worked. Almost the same number of respondents attributed a positive or very positive change in people's values and attitudes and participation in local affairs to the work of the Volunteers.

The odds of a positive change with respect to participation in local affairs were 2.11 times higher among the respondents who had contact with the Volunteers compared to those who had none. The corresponding odds were 1.65 times higher with respect to motivation, 1.30 times higher with respect to cooperation, and 1.17 times higher with respect to values and attitudes.

Using an index of social capital, the differences between the users and beneficiaries of the programme, on the one hand, and the reference group, on the other hand, were also significant, and the biggest differences could be found in areas outside the capital Kathmandu. The index was calculated as an unweighted average of the four different components of social capital used in this study – changes in people's values and attitudes, motivation, cooperation, and participation in local affairs.

A positive impact of the programme was also found with regard to three of the UNDP's four priority areas: the environment, poverty, and jobs. Between half and two-thirds of the users and beneficiaries of the programme considered that the effect of the Volunteers on these areas had been positive or very positive. The odds of indicating positive changes in the environment and on the level of poverty were 2.28 and 2.25 times greater, respectively, among the users and beneficiaries of the programme compared to the reference group. For the availability of jobs, the odds of a positive change were 1.58 times greater among the users and beneficiaries than in the reference group. The biggest positive impact of the programme could be found in small towns and rural areas.

As far as changes in women's lives are concerned, even if almost two-thirds of the respondents indicated that the Volunteers had a positive or very positive effect on women's lives, the changes indicated by the respondents in the reference group were even more positive.

Perceived value of the programme

In terms of the three criteria for measuring the perceived value of the programme, high marks were given on two: the relevance of the programme and the performance of the Volunteers. Room for improvement still exists as far as the third criteria, the sustainability of the results of the work of the Volunteers, is concerned.

The overall conclusion that the programme was relevant during the period covered by the study is based on the fact that almost two-thirds of the respondents rated the relevance of the work of the Volunteers as good or very good. In addition, more than half of the respondents indicated that the Volunteers had done a job that no one else locally could have done. The work of the Volunteers was considered most relevant in areas outside the capital Kathmandu. In the smaller towns and rural areas, the UNV community workers, in particular, were considered to have done a job which no one else could have done locally.

Although a majority of the respondents considered that the results, the continuation, and the long-term benefits of the work of the Volunteers were good or very good, the overall conclusion is that the sustainability of the programme could be improved. This is based on the fact that one in ten of the users and beneficiaries considered that some aspect of sustainability was poor or very poor. One in two of the users and beneficiaries did not think that the continuation of activities was good or very good, and well over half of the respondents did not indicate a lot or very much use of skills or knowledge learned from the Volunteers.

In terms of the performance of the Volunteers, however, the programme faired well. Three out of five rated the effectiveness of the Volunteers good or very good, and more than two-thirds thought the performance of the UN Volunteers in comparison to other volunteers was good or very good. In comparison to international experts, more than half considered that the performance of the Volunteers was good or very good, and less than one in ten thought the performance of the Volunteers was poor or very poor. Compared to other non-nationals, two-thirds of the respondents considered that the performance of the Volunteers was good or very good.

Compared to Nepalese nationals, approximately half of the respondents indicated that the performance of the Volunteers was good or very good. However, almost half of the respondents did not think the performance of the Volunteers in comparison to a Nepalese national was good or very good, and similarly, almost half of the respondents did not think that the Volunteers had done a job that no one else locally could have done.

A conclusion that can be drawn is that even if the performance of the Volunteers overall was considered good, and even very good in a number of cases, the work of the Volunteers may in many cases not have been indispensable. This in particularly seems to have been the case in Kathmandu for the UNV specialists, whose performance in comparison to Nepalese nationals was rated significantly lower than that of the UNV community workers in Kathmandu.

The role of UNV headquarters

Based on the results of this study, the headquarters of the UNV programme can be satisfied with its performance in the past, although room for improvement also does exist. Most of the users and Volunteers expressed satisfaction with the performance of the UNV head office in carrying out its primary functions: the identification of competent and motivated Volunteers, matching of Volunteers with posts, and arranging for the recruitment of the Volunteers. A majority of the respondents were also satisfied with the briefing provided to the host organizations of the Volunteers as well as the language and other training provided to the Volunteers.

Improvements are still possible, in particular with regard to the language training provided to the Volunteers. The normal two-year duration of the assignments of the Volunteers was considered too short by half of the users, who perceived a negative effect on the work of the Volunteers as a consequence. Two other issues, which have been pointed out in previous studies but which this study found needed continuous monitoring, are the availability of co-workers, and the management and supervision of the Volunteers – even if UNV headquarters may have limited ways of influencing these issues.

The monthly living allowance, and to a lesser degree the other benefits, entitlements, and the overall conditions of service, were issues with which a large number of Volunteers expressed dissatisfaction. UNV community workers, in particular, perceived that the living allowance was insufficient, and that this had a negative effect on their work.

The fact that almost half of the UNV community workers said that their living allowance had a negative or very negative effect on their work should, however, not be surprising if one takes into account two things. The first is that UNV specialists receive four or five times what UNV community workers receive; the second is that the total package received by the community workers increased by 15 per cent between 1989 and 1996, while the corresponding increase for UNV specialists was 58 per cent.

A disturbing finding that was made at the outset of the evaluation was the poor quality of the records kept by UNV headquarters. The total number of Volunteer assignments completed in Nepal during the period covered by the study was 110. For 12 of these assignments, the addresses of the Volunteers could not be retrieved, neither at UNV headquarters nor at the UNV office in Kathmandu. Consequently, these 12 Volunteer assignments could not be included in the study. This corresponds to a loss of 11 per cent of potentially useful information.

A related area of concern is the quality of the information available at UNV headquarters and the UNV office in Kathmandu. Very little useful information existed in the reports prepared by the Volunteers on the results or expected results and sustainability of their work, and few records existed of co-workers, supervisors, or beneficiaries of the programme. This would have made an assessment of the work of the Volunteers based on existing records and reports very difficult, even if the reports had been completed and could have been found, which was not the case for almost half of the 110 Volunteer assignments included in the study. This no doubt represents a missed opportunity for collecting and storing relevant information about the programme in an easy and inexpensive way.

In the original sample of fifty Volunteers selected for the study, nine replacements had to be made. Two replacements were unavoidable in order not to risk the safety of the surveyors in areas with political unrest at the time of the survey. Of the other seven Volunteers, three completed less than three months at their assigned duty station, and were substituted because three months was considered too short a period for the Volunteers to have an impact. In these three cases, it can be argued that the programme accepted assignments for Volunteers that were not appropriate or failed to identify and match suitable candidates with posts.

For three other Volunteers, neither co-workers, supervisors, nor any beneficiaries of their work could be found. These assignments were therefore considered failures in terms of the sustainability of the work of the Volunteers. Finally, one Volunteer was substituted because her co-worker refused to be interviewed without an official letter from the UNV programme. This could have been arranged, but was not considered necessary following the receipt of a letter from the Volunteer herself, mailed with a completed questionnaire, that explained major problems in, and the premature termination of, her assignment, which must be considered another failure.

The total failure rate of the programme thus becomes 7 out 50 assignments, or 14 per cent. If this figure is combined with the previous figure of 11 per cent of assignments where it was impossible to even try to locate the Volunteers, the total number of assignments in which the work of the Volunteers had no impact, or no impact could be measured due to lack of proper records, amounts to one-quarter. What this means is that even if the overall satisfaction of the users and the Volunteers with UNV headquarters was very high, it is still possible to improve the performance of the head office.

Other findings

The study also looked at the effect of a number of factors that were considered largely beyond the control of the UNV headquarters, such as links between the activities of the Volunteers and those of other organizations and support provided for the activities of the Volunteers. As could be expected, the effect of links to other organizations and support provided was considered positive by most users of the programme and, even more so, by the Volunteers.

A large majority of the users did not perceive that the external environment had any effect on the work of the Volunteers. Among the Volunteers themselves, somewhat fewer respondents, but still more than half, felt that the external environment had no effect on their performance. Of the external factors, the effects of the political and economic situation were considered negative by the largest number of Volunteers, approximately one-third.

The effect of the UN and government rules and procedures on the work of the Volunteers was considered negative by one in six or seven of the users. Among the Volunteers, one in five thought the rules and procedures of the government had a negative effect on their work. In general, however, the effect of the rules and procedures was not considered important, and some of the Volunteers even thought the effect of the UN and UNV rules and procedures on their work was positive. This may be a reflection of the positive view that many Volunteers had of their link to the UN.

The study also provided an opportunity to compare the assessments of the Volunteers of their achievements and performance with those of their former supervisors, co-workers, and beneficiaries. As could be expected, the estimates of the Volunteers of their own achievements tended in most cases to be higher than the assessments by the users and beneficiaries of the programme. This was particularly the case with the UNV specialists, who estimated their own achievements on average 1.70 times higher than their former supervisors, co-workers, and beneficiaries. For the UNV community workers, the corresponding figure was 1.12.

According to this study, the benefits to the UN Volunteers of participating in the programme were considerable. A vast majority of the UN Volunteers considered that they had learned a lot in terms of new skills and knowledge, and gained a lot in terms of their understanding of another culture. The direct effect of their experience as a UN Volunteer on their next job was, however, less important.

Conclusions and recommendations

A starting point for this study was a proposition that little information exists regarding the performance and achievements of different UN programmes, funds, and agencies and that the different UN organizations therefore should be evaluated to assess the extent to which they achieve their objectives and have an impact.

Future orientation of the UNV programme

The UNV programme was originally established in 1970 to promote the transfer of skills and knowledge to developing countries, and to fill gaps in available human resources, where necessary. Later the mandate of the programme was enlarged to include social capital development, in addition to human capital development. During the period covered by this study, the thematic focus of the programme also included jobs, poverty, women, and the environment – the UNDP's priority areas in the 1980s and 1990s.

What this study shows is that although the programme has been successful in achieving its objectives, significant changes have also taken place without any influence of the UN Volunteers, particularly in the capital Kathmandu. A logical question to ask, therefore, is to what extent the UNV programme should focus more on smaller towns and rural areas where the programme, at least in Nepal, according to this study, has played a more important role? And if this is done, and if there eventually will be less need for the programme in areas outside the capital cities as well, should the programme be closed down, or should the programme look for a new mandate altogether?

An argument could be made that there is much less need for transfer of skills and knowledge today than there was in 1970, because of the ease by which people and ideas move across borders in today's world. Although a commonly held view is that this process gained momentum in the 1990s, it is all the same a process that has been ongoing ever since the UNV programme was established, and something that the programme appears to have been able to respond to. According to two-thirds of the respondents, the relevance of the UNV programme during the period covered by the study was good or very good. One can assume that if the Volunteers in Nepal had been performing the same tasks in the late 1980s and early 1990s as their predecessors were in the 1970s, the ratings would not have been as favourable.

Since 1970, however, a lot has no doubt changed in the world, and certain countries, that 10 or 20 years ago benefited from the assistance of UNV may no longer need the programme to develop the human capacities they require. To some extent, this may also be the case in Nepal, where almost half of the users and beneficiaries of the programme indicated that someone locally could have done the work of the UN Volunteer. In the capital Kathmandu, one-third of the respondents thought the Volunteers did a job that no one else locally could have done; in other areas of Nepal, the corresponding number was two-thirds.

A possible interpretation of the findings of this study could be that the UNV programme may be reaching a point where it has served its purpose in the capital cities, and should now shift its focus to areas outside the capital, until the programme eventually could be phased out completely. Although no UN programme should be expected to continue forever, this seems like a frightening scenario for the UNV programme. This does, however, not need to be the case if another aspect of the programme is taken into consideration and given more prominence. This is the value to the Volunteers from participating in the programme and what has been referred to as the two-way or exchange nature of the programme.

Even if electronic and other forms of communication continue to be developed, the need for exchange programmes, through which people can share experiences and learn from each other through direct contact, will remain important. In addition to the UNV programme and other volunteer sending agencies, many other possibilities for nationals of one country to work in another country exist through other organizations, government programmes, and the private sector. For nationals of many developing countries, however, the UNV programme is one of the few vehicles in the non-profit sector that exist to help them share and gain experiences in another country.

If the benefits to countries of sending as well as receiving Volunteers are taken together, the value of the UNV programme increases. Providing opportunities through the UNV programme for individuals to live and work in another country could also be argued for not only in order to achieve the specific objectives of the programme, but also to promote the broader goals of the UN – peace, justice, and tolerance. This argument was mentioned as early as 1961 in some of the first discussions in ECOSOC on the establishment of the UNV programme, but does not appear to be one of the basic principles of the programme at present.[1]

Defining exchange of knowledge and experience as the *raison d'être* of the UNV programme would not necessarily mean limiting the programme to human or social capital development or priority areas of the UNDP. The programme could continue looking for opportunities to support private sector development, humanitarian relief, peace building, human rights, electoral assistance, or other areas, as circumstances and needs in different countries change. The key would be to provide meaningful opportunities for individuals from different countries or cultures to work together, sharing experiences and learning from each other. If the possibility for nationals of a country to work in their own country as national UN Volunteers is further emphasized, the justifications for the programme become even stronger.

Despite all the changes that have taken place since the creation of the UNV programme, the continuous expansion of the programme, and the constant search for new opportunities, one of the original reasons for the establishment of the programme still seems very valid and relevant today. This is to respond to the desire of individuals to dedicate a period of their lives to the cause of development, and to offer them a positive means of translating their concern for their fellow men into an effective force for economic and social progress throughout the world.

The UN Volunteers as true volunteers

Since its establishment, the UNV programme has had to grapple with two difficult and related issues: the concept of volunteerism and the remuneration of the Volunteers. The perception of volunteers as young, inexperienced, and idealistic has been countered by the programme by stressing the qualifications, experience, and maturity of the UN Volunteers, in addition to their motivation and commitment. In the late 1980s, in an attempt to attract even more qualified and suitable candidates, the monthly living allowance of the UNV specialists was substantially increased and linked to the cost of living in each country. Whether this led to an improvement in the quality of the candidates and the performance of the Volunteers is not clear, since the effects of these changes in the conditions of service were not studied at the time.

What is clear is that the issue of the remuneration of the Volunteers has remained problematic, as is evidenced by the findings of this study. Even if international UN Volunteers are paid much less than international UN staff, UNV specialists earn considerably more than most of the nationals of the country in which they are working. This has led to a perception of them as neither true volunteers nor UN staff. Instead, the UNV specialists, who make up the large majority of the UN Volunteers, are viewed as "cheap labour" or "second class citizens" by many UN staff, while at the same time considered overpaid by many government officials in the countries where they work.

It may indeed be that it was necessary to increase the monthly living allowance in the late 1980s and early 1990s because the pool of qualified candidates was not large enough at that time. Today, however, the situation is very different, as the roster of candidates of the UNV programme also shows. Moreover, shrinking resources for development cooperation overall has led to fewer opportunities to work in developing countries through bilateral or multilateral programmes. This in turn has made the UNV programme more attractive as an option for people looking for opportunities to work in developing countries.

What the UNV programme, therefore, might consider at this point is relying less on, or, if possible, moving completely away from, using the level of the remuneration as a way to attract candidates for UNV specialist assignments. This would, however, require finding other ways of rewarding the Volunteers for their work, showing the Volunteers, and those with whom they work, that their contribution, commitment, and motivation are truly appreciated, even if the rewards in monetary terms are not very high. What would be required is much more than emphasizing the commitment and motivation as the trade mark of the Volunteers, as the programme has in the past.

Simply paying the UNV specialists less, however, is not the solution, and a much broader set of policy changes would be required. These could, however, provide the programme with an opportunity to get away from the existing situation in which the UN Volunteers are neither considered true volunteers nor regular UN staff. A starting point could be viewing the Volunteers as participants in the UNV programme. This would mean not only focusing on what the Volunteers contribute to the programme, but also acknowledging the importance of the UNV assignment to the Volunteers themselves, both during their time as Volunteers and afterwards.

If the value of the former Volunteers to the programme were fully realized, more attention would probably be given to the Volunteers during their assignment. By the end of 2000, more than 20,000 individuals will have served as UN Volunteers, and they will constitute an enormous pool of, largely untapped, potential ambassadors for the UN, the UNV programme, and volunteerism more generally. For many, their experience as a UN Volunteer will be the only one of working with the UN, working in another country, or working as a volunteer. Most will be influenced in their choices and decisions later on in life by their experience as Volunteers, and for some their willingness to help other people, to work as volunteers, or to promote the overall goals of the UN will be shaped by their experience as a UN Volunteer.

Although associations of former Volunteers have been established in a few countries, the UNV programme itself appears to have been unable to utilize former Volunteers to promote volunteerism, the UNV programme, or the broader goals of the UN. A possible explanation could be that many of the former Volunteers never identified very strongly with the UN, the UNV programme, or other volunteers, and using them to promote volunteerism, the UNV programme, or the goals of the UN has, therefore, not worked very well in practice.

Much more could be done for the Volunteers so that they are seen and perceived to be true volunteers – by the Volunteers themselves and by others. This would require giving the Volunteers the respect they deserve and the recognition they need in order to make them willing to give irrespective of the financial remuneration they receive. Even if the monthly allowance paid to the UNV specialists were reduced, the overall terms and conditions of the Volunteers could be further improved. This could, for instance, include helping the Volunteers stay up-to-date in their field by providing access to the Internet, books and journals in their field, and opportunities to participate in conferences and workshops during their assignment.

Given that the total cost of the Volunteer assignments should not increase, doing more for the Volunteers as part of the programme means that it would probably be necessary to reduce the amount currently paid to the UNV specialists. The counter argument to doing more for the Volunteers is that it is better to pay the Volunteers as much as possible, a going market rate, if you will, and let the Volunteers themselves decide how to update or upgrade their skills, etc. Experience from the non-profit sector as well as the private sector, however, shows that using monetary rewards as incentives does not work very well in the long run. Moreover, for the Volunteers to be perceived as true volunteers, the size of their financial remuneration should not be driving either the supply or the demand for Volunteers.

The ideal should be to attract Volunteers because they want to contribute to economic development or the other goals of the UN, not because of the financial benefits they receive from participating in the UNV programme. At a time of continued globalization with persisting, and even increasing, gaps between rich and poor, expressions of solidarity with the less privileged are needed, and the UN should be able to provide opportunities for this through a programme such as the UN Volunteers.

If paying less to the Volunteers does not seem reasonable, the living allowance of the UNV specialists could be decreased, while increasing their resettlement grant. This could be seen as a way of paying the Volunteers a remuneration commensurate to that of a true volunteer, but rewarding them after their assignment for their contribution, motivation, and commitment. This would also smooth the transition from being a UN Volunteer.

The role of the UNV programme within the UN system

The situation in which the UN Volunteers have been perceived as neither true volunteers nor regular UN staff has also blurred the image of the UNV programme and reduced its effectiveness. This study demonstrates that the programme has been able to work with a range of different UN organizations, government institutions, and non-governmental organizations as well as with communities at least since the mid 1980s. It has been successful and appreciated in its work with its non-UN partners, but its influence on other UN organizations appears rather limited.

While this study concludes that the UNV programme has established successful partnerships with what could be referred to as non-traditional partners of the UN, the programme does not appear to have played any role in bringing other UN organizations closer to the non-traditional partners of the UN. Instead, the other programmes, funds, and agencies of the UN have developed their own ways of working with civil society, without using the UNV programme as a bridge or benefiting from the experience of the UNV programme.

The limited influence of the UNV programme on the work of its UN system partners illustrates that as long as the image and status of the UN Volunteers remains unclear, the impact of the programme remains below its potential. In the early 1990s, in what may have been a reaction to a lack of recognition of the programme, the programme began funding its own development projects, ostensibly to promote volunteerism. The real reason, however, may have been to try to demonstrate that the programme could be viewed as a development agency in its own right, not merely as a recruitment arm of UN system.

Although there may be some justification for special UNV projects, it is likely that the efforts of the programme to design and manage its own projects diverted attention and resources away from what could be considered the core functions of the programme. This could explain some of the dissatisfaction of the Volunteers and the users of the programme with the ability of the programme to recruit and match Volunteers with posts, to prepare the Volunteers for their assignments, and to provide them with the necessary support.

While there are a number of multilateral and bilateral programmes and non-governmental organizations with considerable experience of developing and managing projects, few, volunteer sending agencies apart, have extensive experience in the area in which the UNV programme originally was set up: recruitment. Recruitment of personnel may not be as exciting as management of projects, but its importance should not be underestimated or undervalued. As long as the development cooperation efforts of the UN include a personnel component, the recruitment of qualified, committed, motivated, and suitable individuals remains extremely important, irrespective of whether the individuals are volunteers or not. The UNV programme can perform this function and provide a service to other UN organizations and governments that is needed to complement the work of the other UN programmes, funds, and agencies, to make the development cooperation efforts of the UN as a whole more effective.

A conclusion of this study is that the programme should focus on the function that it was originally established to do and that it probably does best, recruitment of Volunteers, and continue trying to do this even better. In this way the UNV programme could best support the development cooperation efforts of the UN system as a whole. This applies irrespective of whether the programme is able to come to terms with the issue of the UN Volunteers as true volunteers or not. However, if the term "Volunteer" remains a misnomer, it might be better to rename the UN Volunteers as UN Aid Workers, UN Development Workers, UN Relief Workers, or something similar. This would acknowledge that the individuals recruited through the programme may be qualified, committed, motivated, and suitable, but that they are not volunteers in the sense usually understood as people doing something for little or no financial reward.

Need for improved documentation

Whereas the overall conclusion of this study is that the programme has had an impact and is appreciated, improvements could be made, particularly in the area of documentation. In this area a lot could be achieved with little effort, and little or no additional costs. Although access to all records of the programme was provided for this study, an enormous amount of effort had to go into trying to identify respondents for the survey and to retrieve records, which in many cases could not be found. When records could be found, the quality of the information contained in them left a lot to be desired.

To deal with the problem of inadequate documentation, two issues could be addressed at the same time. The first is collecting more relevant information from the Volunteers in the countries where they work; the second is keeping better records at the headquarters of the programme. Very little would be required to have the Volunteers list supervisors, co-workers, and beneficiaries in their periodic reports. A somewhat more challenging task would be asking the Volunteers to collect baseline data of objective indicators of development against which it would be possible to measure overall changes and outcomes of their work.

Different indicators and benchmarks would be needed in different fields of work – to assist the Volunteers, the head office of the programme would need to provide examples that could be used in different fields in different countries. Yet more time consuming, but also possible to do at the outset of a Volunteer assignment, with some guidance and training, would be the identification of individuals who could constitute a control group.

Listing beneficiaries, collecting data on indicators of change, and establishing control groups, where possible, would allow for a comparison of a situation before a Volunteer took up his or her assignment with the situation after his or her departure. This would make future impact assessments much easier and faster to carry out. In this study, the data collection and analysis alone took more than a year and a half to complete by one full-time researcher, fourteen surveyors who carried out the interviews with the backing of a Nepalese NGO, and four research assistant who compiled the background data and coded the survey data.

In addition to facilitating future research, better records, baseline data, objective indicators, and control groups would also allow for the use of more robust research designs in future evaluations. Although the relationship between time, costs, and complexity of a study, on the one hand, and the usefulness of the results, on the other hand, need to be kept in mind, in certain instances, for selected countries, more costly and more time-consuming longitudinal or quasi-experimental studies could be considered. Beneficiaries could also be involved in the design and implementation of evaluations of this kind. Finally, the establishment of control groups at the outset would also allow for the use of other methods, such as productivity comparisons, to determine the impact of the work of the Volunteers.

Value of the study and suggestions for future research

For the UNV programme, this study was a first assessment of its impact, and many lessons can be learned from it. Compared to previous evaluations of the programme, the study was different in four important respects.

The first difference is that the study assessed the impact of the work of UN Volunteers a few years after the Volunteers had left, which almost by definition is required of an impact assessment.

A second difference is that the study was based on the responses of a relatively large number of individuals (169) who had first-hand experience of the work of specific Volunteers. In the past, evaluations were based on the views of a handful of government and UN officials of the performance of the UNV headquarters and the work of the Volunteers in general.

A third difference was that results of the work of the Volunteers were compared to changes that had taken place without any involvement of the Volunteers, that is, a "counterfactual situation". The performance of the Volunteers was also compared to others who, at least in theory, could have been recruited to do the same job as the Volunteers.

The fourth difference was that information was collected from users and beneficiaries of the programme as well as from the Volunteers themselves. This made it possible to determine how much the Volunteers' assessments of their own achievements and performance differed from those of their former supervisors, co-workers, and beneficiaries.

What this study has confirmed is that it is possible to carry out an assessment of the impact of a programme, such as the UNV programme, that does not produce physical outputs, and that the results of an assessment of this kind can provide useful information about the programme. What the study has also shown that there is a need for more rapid and economical ways of assessing the impact of the UNV or any other UN programme.

As far as the methodology of the study is concerned, the approach of combining different sources of information, reports by Volunteers and external evaluators, interviews, and a mail survey, can be considered very useful. This approach can be recommended for future research, as can using locally hired surveyors to carry out the data collection. The survey instruments that were developed for the study can also be used, with minor modifications, in future evaluations. By arriving at an estimate of the extent by which the Volunteers' estimates of their performance differed from those of their supervisors, co-workers, and beneficiaries, this study has also laid the ground for future assessments of the impact of the UNV programme based on self-evaluations by the Volunteers.

This study provides many useful insights to the programme, but cannot explain what determines the effectiveness or success of individual Volunteers, or how different factors and circumstances influence the work of the Volunteers, or, ultimately, the impact of the programme. This will require further research, for which the conceptual framework used in this study can provide a starting point.

There are also valuable lessons to be learned from this study for other UN programmes. Even if the UN Volunteers are thought of as a distinct category within the UN, the work the Volunteers does often not differ significantly from that of other UN staff. Increasingly, in fact, UN Volunteers are doing jobs that other staff of UN agencies used to do in the past. The methodology used in this study could therefore equally well be used for assessments of other UN funds, programmes, and agencies. The most direct application of the approach used in this study would be assessments of the impact of training programmes, such as on-the-job training. However, the study also showed that the methodology can be used to assess the impact of a programme on a variety of different areas, such as job availability, poverty, women's lives, and the environment.

In the end, there are at least four lessons to be learned for other UN funds, programmes, and agencies.

1. Existing records and data are likely to be of little use for an impact study, and collection of original data probably becomes necessary.

2. Carrying out an impact evaluation without both pre- and post-intervention assessments and a control group, in the true sense of the term, is possible but is both costly and time consuming.

3. Relating achievements of a programme to objective indicators of development is recommended to further strengthen the design of an impact evaluation.

4. The importance of collecting baseline data, identifying beneficiaries, and establishing control groups at the outset of programmes or projects cannot be emphasized enough to enable monitoring of progress and to facilitate future impact assessments.

Note

1. See Economic and Social Council Document E/3548. "Use of Volunteer Workers in the Operational Programmes of the United Nations and Related Agencies Designed to Assist in the Economic and Social Development of the Less Developed Countries". 3 August 1961; and United Nations Volunteers. *Strategy 2000*. Bonn: UNV, 1997.

Appendix A

Details of the impact of the UNV programme

The assessment of the impact of the UNV programme was made based on the following criteria: changes in human capital, changes in social capital, and changes with respect to the UNDP's four priority areas, that is, jobs, poverty, the environment, and women's lives.

Changes in human capital

To assess changes in human capital, respondents were asked to list new skills or knowledge that they, or others in their communities or workplace, had learned. The responses of the 169 users and beneficiaries of the programme to the question whether the Volunteers had taught them any new skills or knowledge are shown in Figure A.1. The total number of missing responses was 4 out of 169. These 4 respondents, 2.4 per cent, gave "do not know" as an answer. Missing responses are not included in this graph, or any of the subsequent graphs.

9.7 per cent of the respondents indicated that the Volunteers had not taught them any new skills or knowledge, 12.7 per cent said that they had acquired one new skill or area of knowledge from the Volunteers. 24.2, 19.4, and 20.0 per cent, a total of 63.6 per cent, of the respondents indicated two, three, or four, respectively, as the number of new skills or areas in which they had learned new knowledge from the Volunteers. 10.3 per cent indicated five, 1.8 per

Figure A.1 Number of new skills or areas in which new
knowledge was learned by the users and
beneficiaries

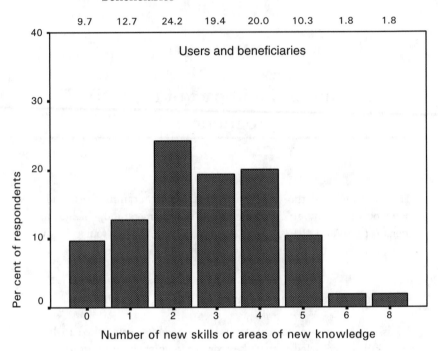

Number of new skills or areas of new knowledge

cent indicated six, and another 1.8 per cent indicated eight as the
number of new skills or areas in which they had acquired knowledge
from the Volunteers.

The responses of the reference group to the corresponding question, that is, whether people in their ministry, department, project,
or community had learned any new skills or knowledge over the last
5 to 10 years are shown in Figure A.2.

11.3 per cent of the respondents in the reference group indicated
that they had not learned any new skills or knowledge, while 18.9
per cent said that they had learned one new skill or area of knowledge. 33.0, 19.8, and 11.3 per cent, a total of 64.1 per cent, of the
respondents indicated two, three, or four, respectively, as the number
of new skills or areas in which they had learned new knowledge. 1.9

Figure A.2 Number of new skills or areas in which new
knowledge was learned by the reference group

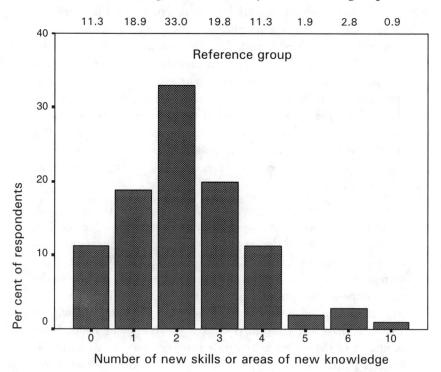

Number of new skills or areas of new knowledge

per cent indicated five, 2.8 per cent indicated six, and 0.9 per cent
indicated ten as the number of skills or areas in which they had acquired new knowledge. The total number of missing responses was
23, or 17.8 per cent out of a total of 129. 13 of these respondents
had wrongly focused their response on an institution other than the
one where the Volunteer concerned had worked, and their responses
were therefore excluded. The other 10 respondents gave either no
answer or responded "do not know" to the question.

Significance of results

Among the users and beneficiaries as well as in the reference group,
approximately 10 per cent of all the respondents indicated that no

accumulation of skills or knowledge had taken place. Slightly more than one-third of the users and beneficiaries (37.0 per cent) and slightly more than a half of the reference group (51.9 per cent) indicated one or two as the number of skills learned or areas in which they had acquired new knowledge. Approximately half of the users and beneficiaries (53.3 per cent) and slightly more than one-third of the respondents in the reference group (36.8 per cent) indicated three or more as the number of new skills learned or areas in which they had acquired new knowledge. If the number of respondents are counted who gave four or more as the number of skills learned or areas in which they had learned new knowledge, these represented 33.9 per cent of the users and beneficiaries and 17.0 per cent of the reference group.

Among the users and beneficiaries, the average number of skills learned or areas in which they had learned new knowledge was 2.8, the median was 3 and the mode 2. In the reference group, the average was 2.2, the median was 2 and the mode 2. The difference in the average number of new skills or areas of knowledge learned in the two groups was statistically significant ($p = 0.013$). Based on these and the figures presented above, some more skills and knowledge appear to have been acquired among the users and beneficiaries compared to the reference group. It may, however, be that the differences in the number of new skills or knowledge learned reflect differences in the age, education, gender, or geographical location of the respondents, or something else rather than interaction with the Volunteers.

A multiple regression analysis was therefore performed to test if the interaction with the Volunteers could explain the differences in the number of new skills and knowledge learned by different respondents. Contact with the Volunteers and four other explanatory variables were included in the analysis: the age, gender, and education of the respondents as well as their geographical location. The linear combination of the five explanatory variables was significantly related to the number of new skills or knowledge learned: $F(5,264) = 12.70$, $p = 0.000$. The multiple correlation coefficient was 0.44, indicating that approximately 18 per cent of the variance in the number of new skills or knowledge learned could be accounted for by the combination of the five explanatory variables. A statistically significant difference between the two groups of respondents could be found with respect to the geographical location of the respondents ($p = 0.000$). This result indicates that the number of new skills or knowledge learned outside the capital Kathmandu was greater than in the capital.

In terms of the number of new skills or knowledge learned, the difference between the respondents who had interacted with the Volunteers and those who did not have any contact with the Volunteers was not statistically significant ($p = 0.118$). A possible explanation could be that respondents in the reference group learned new skills and knowledge from individuals who in turn had acquired these through their interaction with the Volunteers, but this is not likely. The reason is that the skills and knowledge that the respondents in the reference group listed were, in most cases, different from those stated by the users and beneficiaries of the programme.

The multiple regression analysis presented above was also performed excluding cases pair-wise instead of list-wise, – list-wise was used as the default procedure in this study. The pair-wise exclusion procedure entails using all cases for which complete data exists for the pair of variables being correlated to compute the correlation co-efficient on which, for instance, a regression analysis is based. The degrees of freedom are based on the minimum pair-wise number of observations. In this case the difference in the number of new skills or knowledge learned by the respondents who had contact and those who did not have any contact with the Volunteers was almost statistically significant ($p = 0.060$). Further analyses were therefore considered necessary before drawing any conclusions regarding the impact of the UNV programme on the transfer of skills and knowledge.

A simple factorial analysis of variance (ANOVA) procedure was used to assess the effect of the interaction between the respondents' age, education, gender, geographical location, and contact with the Volunteers on the number of new skills or knowledge learned. Three of the ten interaction effects were statistically significant: the interaction between the age and education of the respondents ($p = 0.047$), between the education and geographical location of the respondents ($p = 0.036$), and between the geographical location and the contact with the Volunteers ($p = 0.000$).

Of the three interaction effects, the last one is of most interest to this study, and formed the basis for performing a multiple regression analysis in which an interaction term in the form of geographical location times contact with the Volunteers was introduced. The age, gender, education, and geographical location of the respondents, and contact with the Volunteers were included as the other explanatory variables.

The linear combination of these variables remained significantly related to the number of new skills or knowledge learned, $F(6,263) = 12.95$, $p = 0.000$, and the explanatory power of the regression analysis increased with the introduction of the interaction term to $R = 0.48$ (compared to 0.44 without the interaction term), indicating that approximately 21 per cent (previously 18 per cent) of the variance in the number of new skills or knowledge learned could be accounted for by the combination of the explanatory variables.

The results of the regression analysis with an interaction term included indicated that the effect of the interaction between the geographical location and the contact with the Volunteers was statistically significant ($p = 0.001$). Further analyses included interpreting the significance of the interaction effect within a regression analysis framework using t-tests, as well as analysis of variance and F-tests for the different sub-groups of respondents that corresponded to the interaction between geographical location and contact with the Volunteers. The results of both analyses were very similar.

The average number of new skills or areas of knowledge learned by the users and beneficiaries of the programme in Kathmandu was smaller than the corresponding number in the reference group in Kathmandu, but the difference was not statistically significant ($p = 0.131$). In other areas of Nepal, however, the users and beneficiaries indicated a significantly greater number of skills and more new knowledge acquired than the reference group ($p = 0.001$). Users and beneficiaries of the programme in areas outside Kathmandu also indicated significantly more new skills or knowledge learned than the users and beneficiaries in Kathmandu ($p = 0.000$).

What the results above indicate is that the programme, in terms of transfer of skills and knowledge, appears to have been most effective in areas outside the capital Kathmandu. It may be that the types of jobs performed by the Volunteers in Kathmandu were quite different from those performed by the Volunteers outside the capital, or that the existing level of human capital to start with was higher in Kathmandu than in other areas. This does, however, not alter the basic finding that the programme seems to have been most successful in terms of human capital development in areas outside Kathmandu.

A review of the skills and knowledge transferred shows that the skills and knowledge acquired by the respondents were very different in terms of their nature and difficult to compare in terms of their importance. This confirmed the limitation of the number of new skills or knowledge as an indicator of human capital, which was known from the outset. It was, therefore, considered necessary to perform additional analyses before drawing any further conclusions regarding the impact of the work of the Volunteers on human capital accumulation.

To further analyse the impact of the UNV programme on human capital, a logistic regression analysis was performed. In this analysis the impact on human capital was considered *minor* if the respondents had indicated zero to two as the number of skills learned or areas in which they had learned new knowledge. The impact was considered *major* if the respondents had indicated three or more as the number of skills learned or areas in which they had learned new knowledge. The decision to group the responses in these two categories was made based on the nature of the skills and knowledge listed by the respondents and the frequency distribution of the responses. Five dichotomous covariates were included in the analysis: the age, gender, and education of the respondents, the geographical location, and contact with the Volunteers.

The *odds* of a major change in human capital is defined as the probability of a major change in human capital over the probability of a minor change in human capital (when different covariates change values from zero to one). For the variable of most interest to this study, contact with the Volunteers, the odds of a major change in human capital increased by a factor of 1.80 when a respondent had contact with a Volunteer, all other things held constant.

The *Wald* statistic in the logistic regression analysis was used to test the hypothesis that interaction with the Volunteers leads to greater positive changes in human capital. Based on the significance of the *Wald* statistic in the case above $(p = 0.047)$, the null hypothesis, that the respondents who did not have contact with the Volunteers exhibited a greater change in human capital, can be rejected. The R statistic $(-1 < R < 1)$, albeit small (0.072), also indicates that the likelihood of a major change in human capital was greater among the users and beneficiaries of the programme than in the reference group.

Based on the results of the logistic regression analysis presented above, the UNV programme thus appears to have had a positive effect on human capital that is greater than the corresponding change in the reference group. If an interaction term is included in the analysis, as was done with the multiple regression analysis, the difference is even more evident, particularly in areas outside the capital Kathmandu. A note of caution is, however, needed since the results to some extent depend on how a change in human capital is defined. The limitations of the number of new skills or areas of knowledge as an indicator of human capital also need to be kept in mind.

If a major change in human capital is defined as the acquisition of 3–10 or 4–10 new skills or knowledge in 3–10 or 4–10 areas, the change in human capital among the users and beneficiaries is significantly greater than in the reference group. If a major change is defined as acquisition of 2–10 new skills or knowledge in 2–10 areas, the difference between the users and beneficiaries and the reference group is not statistically significant $(p = 0.292)$. The odds of a major change in human capital accumulation are still 1.39 times greater if a respondent interacted with a Volunteer. Once the analysis is performed with no acquisition of new skills or knowledge as one value, and acquisition of 1–10 new skills or knowledge in 1–10 areas as the other value, the difference between the users and beneficiaries and the reference group is not significant ($p = 0.906$). In this case, the odds of acquiring skills and knowledge are actually somewhat smaller (by a factor of 0.95) if a respondent had contact with a Volunteer.

Finally, in the analysis presented above, for one other covariate, the location of the respondents, the *Wald* statistic was also significant ($p = 0.000$). In this case the odds of a major change in human capital decrease by a factor of 0.19 when a respondent from an area outside the capital is substituted by a respondent from the capital Kathmandu. Expressed in another way, the odds of a major change in human capital increase by a factor of 5.28 when a respondent from the capital Kathmandu is replaced by a respondent from an area outside the capital.

Changes in social capital

The second objective of the study focused on changes in social capital in communities or organizations where UN Volunteers worked. The components of social capital that were measured included people's values and attitudes, motivation, cooperation, and participation in local affairs.

Changes in values and attitudes

The way the users and beneficiaries of the programme perceived that the Volunteers had affected the values and attitudes of people in the communities or organizations where they worked is shown in Figure A.3.

One respondent (0.6 per cent) perceived that the Volunteer had negatively influenced the values and attitudes of people with whom the Volunteer had worked. 21.5 per cent of the respondents thought the Volunteers did not change the values or attitudes in any way.

Figure A.3 Perceived effect of the Volunteers on the values and attitudes of people

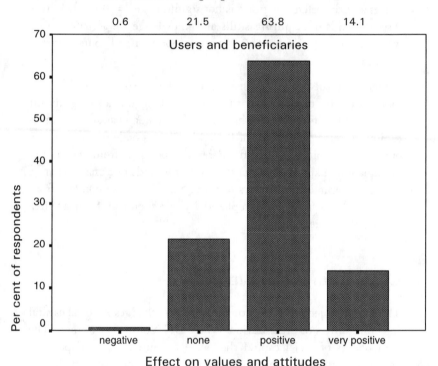

63.8 per cent of the respondents indicated that the Volunteers had positively influenced the values and attitudes. Another 14.1 per cent felt that the Volunteers had a very positive influence on the values and the attitudes of people with whom they had worked. Of the total 169 respondents, 3.6 per cent gave "do not know" or no answer to the question.

Motivation and cooperation

The perceived effect of the Volunteers on the motivation and cooperation among people in the communities or organizations where they worked can be seen in Figures A.4 and A.5.

Figure A.4 Perceived effect of the Volunteers on the motivation of people

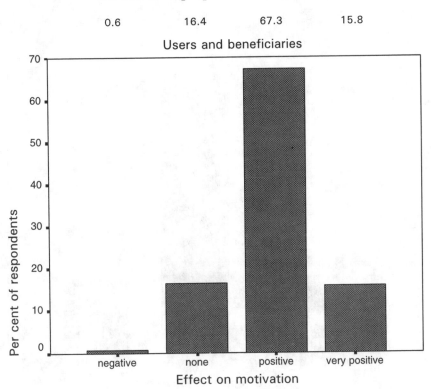

One respondent (0.6 per cent) thought the Volunteer had changed the motivation of people in a negative way. 16.4 per cent did not think the Volunteers had changed the motivation of people at all. 67.3 per cent considered that the Volunteers had changed the motivation of people in the community or organization where they worked in a positive way. Another 15.8 per cent indicated that the Volunteers had influenced the motivation of people in a very positive way. 2.4 per cent indicated "do not know" as an answer.

16.7 per cent of the respondents thought that the Volunteers did not have any effect on the cooperation among people. 66.0 per cent of the respondents considered that the Volunteers had changed the

Figure A.5 Perceived effect of the Volunteers on the cooperation of people

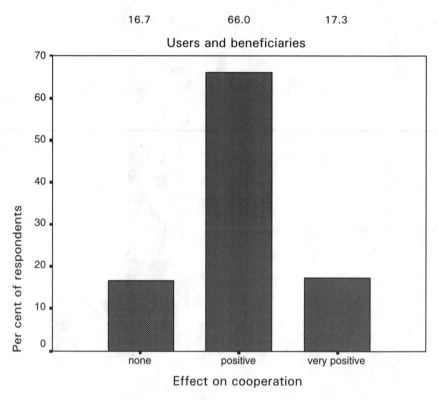

cooperation among people in the community or organization where they worked in a positive way. 17.3 per cent indicated a very positive effect of the work of the Volunteers on cooperation. 7 of the 169 respondents, or 4.1 per cent, said they did not know if the Volunteers had changed the cooperation among people.

Participation

The perceived influence of the Volunteers on people's participation in local affairs is shown in Figure A.6.

Figure A.6 Perceived effect of the Volunteers on people's participation

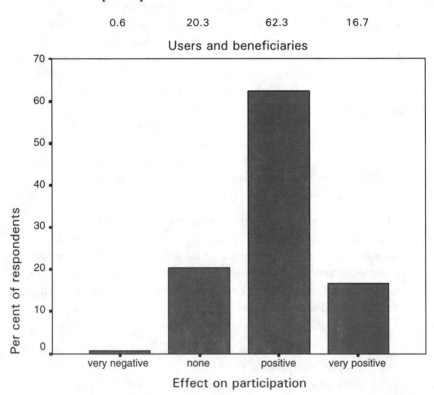

One respondent (0.6 per cent) thought there was a very negative change in the participation of people in the activities of the local community as a result of the work of the Volunteer concerned. 20.3 per cent did not think that the work of the Volunteers led to any change in local participation. 62.3 per cent of the respondents considered that a positive change in the participation of people in the activities of the local community was an outcome of the work of the Volunteers. 16.7 per cent of the respondents indicated a very positive influence on people's participation as an outcome of the work of the Volunteers. 3.6 per cent of the respondents gave "do not know" as an answer.

Significance of results

One in every five or six of the respondents (between 16.7 and 21.7 per cent) thought the Volunteers had no effect or a negative effect on the different components of social capital. At the most, one respondent (0.6 per cent) considered the effect negative or very negative. More than four out of five of the respondents thought that the Volunteers had a positive or very positive influence on the motivation and cooperation of people in the community or organization where they worked (83.0 and 83.3 per cent, respectively). Almost four out of five of the respondents also attributed a positive or very positive change in people's values and attitudes, and in people's participation in the activities of the local community, to the work of the Volunteers (78.3 and 79.0 per cent, respectively).

Based on the results presented above, the Volunteers seem to have had a considerable positive impact on social capital. However, to ascertain this, two things needed to be done. Firstly, the responses of the users and beneficiaries of the programme were compared to those of the reference group, and secondly, the different components of social capital were combined together to get an overall assessment of the impact of the programme on social capital.

To assess the differences between the responses of the users and beneficiaries of the programme and those of the reference group, multiple regression analyses with respect to each of the four components of social capital were performed. For three of the components, changes in people's motivation, cooperation, and participation in local affairs, there was a statistically significant difference in favour of the respondents who had interacted with the Volunteers ($0.004 < p < 0.023$). For the fourth component, changes in values and attitudes, the difference between the responses of those who had contact and those who had no contact with the Volunteers was not statistically significant ($p = 0.123$).

Given that the perceptions of the respondents with respect to changes in the components of social capital were very well represented by two categories, logistic regression analysis was also considered appropriate to compare the responses of the users and beneficiaries of the programme and the reference group. Some information was, however, inevitably lost when the responses were collapsed into two values. The two values used in the logistic regression analyses of changes in the components of social capital were "none or negative" and "positive". Five dichotomous covariates were included in the analyses: the age, gender, and education of the respondents, the geographical location, and contact with the Volunteers.

The logistic regression analyses showed that the *odds* of a positive change in people's values and attitudes increased by a factor of 1.17 when a respondent had contact with a Volunteer, all other things held constant. The difference between the users and beneficiaries and the reference group, however, was not significant ($p = 0.610$, $R = 0.000$). In the case of people's motivation, the *odds* of a positive change in motivation increased by a factor of 1.65 when a respondent had contact with a Volunteer, all other things being equal. The difference between the users and beneficiaries and the reference group was not significant ($p = 0.121$), but the R statistic (0.038) indicated a greater likelihood of a positive change in the motivation among the users and beneficiaries of the programme than in the reference group.

In terms of cooperation among people, the *odds* of a positive change in cooperation increased by a factor of 1.30 when a respondent had contact with a Volunteer, all other things held constant. The difference between the users and beneficiaries and the reference group was, however, not significant ($p = 0.439$, $R = 0.000$). For people's participation, the *odds* of a positive change in people's participation increased by a factor of 2.11 when a respondent had contact with a Volunteer, all other things being equal. The difference between the users and beneficiaries and the reference group was, however, not significant ($p = 0.168$, $R = 0.000$).

In summary, the results of the logistic regression analyses of the individual components of social capital were consistent with the multiple regression analyses presented above, but do not provide any additional information regarding the impact of the UNV programme on the individual components of social capital.

To get an overall assessment of the impact of the programme on social capital, an index of change in social capital was calculated for each respondent. The index was calculated as an unweighted average of the four different components of social capital: change in people's values and attitudes, motivation, cooperation, and participation in local affairs. For the users and beneficiaries, the social capital index mean was 1.90, and for the reference group the mean was 1.60. The difference in the means of the two groups was statistically significant ($p = 0.017$).

A multiple regression analysis was performed to test if interaction with the Volunteers could explain the difference between the two groups of respondents in the change in social capital. Contact with Volunteers and four other explanatory variables were included in the analysis: the age, gender, and education of the respondents as well as their geographical location. The linear combination of these variables was significantly related the social capital index, $F(5,286) = 11.46$, $p = 0.000$. The multiple correlation coefficient was 0.41, indicating that approximately 15 per cent of the variance in the social capital index could be accounted for by the combination of the five explanatory variables.

In terms of the social capital index, a statistically significant difference could be found between the respondents who had interacted with the Volunteers and those who had not had any contact with the Volunteers ($p = 0.002$). This further supports the findings indicating that the Volunteers had a positive impact on social capital. Other statistically significant results could be found with respect to the education of the respondents ($p = 0.000$), and the geographical location ($p = 0.000$). These results indicate that the most significant positive changes in social capital could be found among the respondents who had less formal education and those who worked outside the capital Kathmandu.

A simple factorial ANOVA procedure was used to assess the effect of the interaction between the respondents' age, education, gender, geographical location, and contact with the Volunteers on social capital. Only one of the ten interaction effects was statistically significant: the interaction between the gender and the geographical location of the respondents ($p = 0.018$). The interaction effect between the geographical location and contact with the Volunteers was almost statistically significant ($p = 0.068$); given this, additional analyses of the urban–rural dimension were performed. These included analysing the differences in the assessments of the users and beneficiaries and the reference group respondents in Kathmandu and other areas of Nepal.

In Kathmandu, the average change in social capital among the users and beneficiaries of the programme was greater than the corresponding change in the reference group, but the difference was not statistically significant ($p = 0.366$). In other areas of Nepal, however, the users and beneficiaries indicated a significantly greater increase in social capital than the reference group ($p = 0.033$). In areas outside Kathmandu, both the users and beneficiaries and the reference group respondents indicated a significantly greater increase in social capital than the corresponding groups in Kathmandu ($p = 0.000$ and $p = 0.002$, respectively).

In summary, the results relating to change in social capital are similar to those pertaining to human capital development, and indicate that the UNV programme, in terms of social capital development, also appears to have been most successful in areas outside the capital Kathmandu.

Changes in jobs, poverty, the environment, and women's lives

To measure other outcomes of the work of the Volunteers, in addition to human and social capital formation, the effect of the Volunteers was assessed on the priority areas of the UNDP: job creation, poverty reduction, environmental protection, and advancement of women.

Figure A.7 Perceived effect of the Volunteers on the availability of jobs

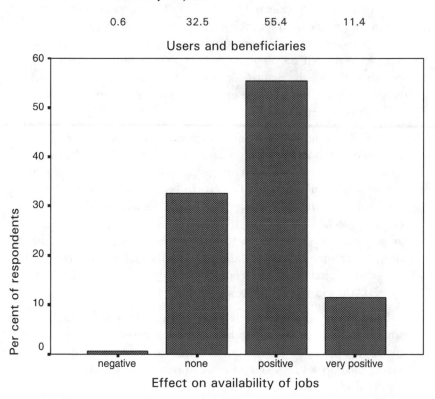

Effects on jobs

The views of the users and beneficiaries on the effect of the Volunteers on the availability of jobs are shown in Figure A.7.

One respondent (0.6 per cent) thought that the Volunteer had a negative effect on the availability of jobs. 32.5 per cent of the respondents did not think that the Volunteers had any effect on jobs. 55.4 per cent of the respondents thought the Volunteers had a positive effect, and 11.4 per cent said the Volunteers had a very positive

Figure A.8 Perceived effect of the Volunteers on the level of poverty

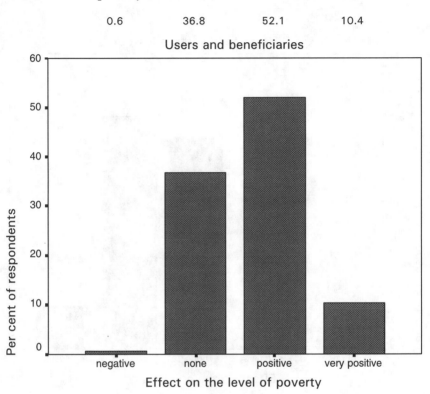

effect on jobs. Of the 169 respondents, 3 (1.8 per cent) gave "do not know" as an answer.

Effects on poverty

The assessment of the users and beneficiaries of the effect of the Volunteers on poverty is shown in Figure A.8.

One respondent (0.6 per cent) said the Volunteer had a negative effect on the level of poverty. 36.8 per cent of the respondents said

Figure A.9 Perceived effect of the Volunteers on the environment

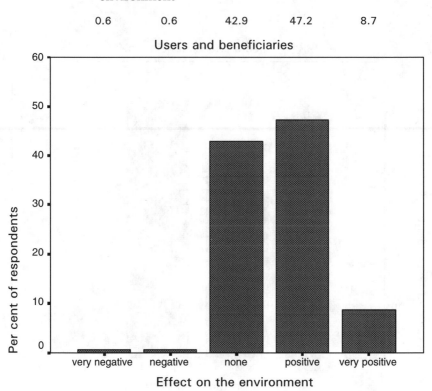

that the Volunteers did not have any effect on the level of poverty, 52.1 per cent of the respondents thought the Volunteers had a positive effect on the level of poverty. 10.4 per cent thought the effect of the Volunteers on the level of poverty was very positive. 3.6 per cent gave "do not know" as an answer.

Effects on the environment

The perceptions of the users and beneficiaries of the effect of the work of the Volunteers on the environment are shown in Figure A.9.

One respondent (0.6 per cent) thought the Volunteers had a very negative effect on the environment and another respondent thought the Volunteers had a negative effect on the environment. 42.9 per cent of the respondents did not think the work of the Volunteers had any effect on the environment. 47.2 per cent of the respondents considered that the Volunteers had a positive effect on the environment and 8.7 per cent thought the effect was very positive. 4.7 per cent of the respondents gave "do not know" as the answer.

Effects on women's lives

The impression of the users and beneficiaries of the effect of the Volunteers on women's lives is given in Figure A.10.

One respondent (0.6 per cent) thought the Volunteer had a negative effect on women's lives. 35.1 per cent of the respondents did not think the Volunteers had any effect on women's lives. 52.6 per cent considered that the Volunteers had a positive effect on women lives and 11.7 per cent thought the volunteers had a very positive effect on women's lives. 15 respondents (8.9 per cent) said they did not know if the Volunteers had any effect on women's lives.

Significance of results

Between one-third and a half of the respondents (33.1 to 44.1 per cent) thought the Volunteers had no effect or a negative effect on the UNDP s priority areas: jobs, poverty, environment, and women. Of these, one, or at the most two, respondents (0.6 or 1.2 per cent) thought the effect was negative or very negative. Approximately two-thirds of the respondents thought the Volunteers had a positive or very positive effect on jobs (66.9 per cent), the level of poverty (62.6 per cent), and women's lives (64.3 per cent). More than one in two (55.9 per cent) thought the Volunteers had a positive or very positive effect on the environment.

To determine the significance of the results described above, the responses of the users and beneficiaries were compared to those of the

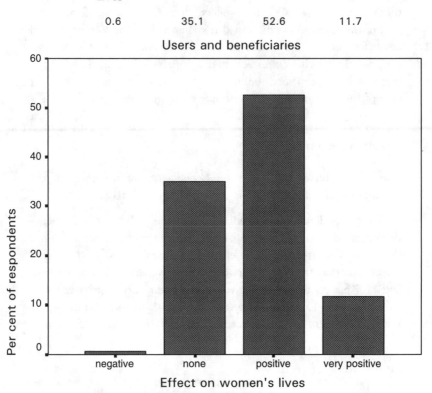

Figure A.10 Perceived effect of the Volunteers on women's
lives

reference group through multiple linear regression analyses with changes in jobs, poverty, the environment, or women's lives as the outcome variables. Five explanatory variables were included in the analyses: the age, gender, and education of the respondents, the geographical location, and the contact with the Volunteers.

In all of the multiple regression analyses, the difference between the respondents who had contact with the Volunteers and those who did not was statistically significant ($p = 0.000$). For three of the areas measured, changes in the availability of jobs, the level of poverty, and the environment, there was a statistically significant difference in favour of the respondents who had interacted with the Volunteers. For the fourth area of interest, changes in women's lives, the respondents who had no contact with the Volunteers indicated a bigger positive change in women's lives than those who had interacted with the Volunteers.

The multiple regression analyses also showed that the biggest positive changes tended to be indicated by younger respondents, respondents with less education, and respondents in areas outside Kathmandu. The only question in which there was a significant difference in the perception of male and female respondents was the one that assessed changes in women's lives. In this particular case, male respondents thought bigger positive changes had taken place in women's lives than did female respondents.

A multiple regression analysis based on an overall index of changes in the UNDP's four priority areas also indicated more positive changes among the users and beneficiaries of the programme than in the reference group. The index was calculated for each respondent as an unweighted average of the four separate areas of focus: jobs, poverty, the environment, and women's lives. Considering, however, that combining the different areas of focus into a single index may indicate little else except that the UN Volunteers contributed to change, additional analyses were considered necessary. Taking into account the fact that the actual responses were very well represented by two categories, logistic regression analysis was considered an appropriate procedure to further analyse the differences in the responses of the users and beneficiaries of the programme and the reference group.

The two values or categories used in the logistic regression analyses of changes in the UNDP's four priority areas were "none or negative" and "positive". Five dichotomous covariates were included in the analyses: the age, gender, and education of the respondents, the geographical location, and contact with the Volunteers.

The logistic regression analyses showed that the *odds* of a positive change in the availability of jobs increased by a factor of 1.58 when a respondent had contact with a Volunteer, all other things held constant. The *Wald* statistic is almost significant ($p = 0.093$), which implies that respondents who had contact with the Volunteers indicated more positive changes in the availability of jobs than those who did not have contact with the Volunteers. The R statistic (0.046) also indicates a greater likelihood of a positive change in job availability among the users and beneficiaries of the programme than in the reference group.

As far as a change in the level of poverty is concerned, the *odds* of a positive change increased by a factor of 2.25 when a respondent had contact with a Volunteer, all other things being equal. Respondents who had contact with Volunteers indicated significantly more positive changes in the level of poverty than those who did not have contact with the Volunteers ($p = 0.004, R = 0.127$).

In the case of a change in the environment, the *odds* of a positive change increased by a factor of 2.28 when a respondent had contact with a Volunteer, all other things held constant. Respondents who had contact with Volunteers indicated significantly more positive changes in the environment than those who did not have contact with the Volunteers ($p = 0.002, R = 0.134$).

In the case women's lives, the *odds* of a positive change decreased by a factor of 0.16 when a respondent had contact with a Volunteer, all other things being equal. In this case respondents who had no contact with the Volunteers indicated more positive changes in women's lives than those who had contact with the Volunteers ($p = 0.000$, and the B coefficient is negative). The R statistic (-0.275), indicates a smaller likelihood of a positive change in women's lives among the users and beneficiaries of the programme than in the reference group.

In summary, the results of the logistic regression analyses of the changes in the UNDP's priority areas were entirely consistent with the multiple regression analyses discussed above, and provide additional support for an overall conclusion of a positive impact of the UNV programme on jobs, poverty, and the environment.

To take the analysis one final step further, the interaction effects between the different explanatory variables for each of the UNDP's four priority areas were reviewed. In the case of changes in the availability of jobs, and changes in the level of poverty, none of the interaction effects was significant. With regard to changes in the environment, there was a significant two-way interaction effect between the age, gender, education of the respondents, and their contact with the Volunteers. As far as changes in women's lives are concerned, the interaction effect between the education of the respondents and their contact with the Volunteers was significant.

A closer look at different groups and sub-groups of respondents showed significant differences between users and beneficiaries and the reference group in Kathmandu as well as in areas outside the capital. The differences in the changes in job availability, poverty, and the environment indicated by the users and beneficiaries in areas outside Kathmandu and those indicated by the users and beneficiaries in Kathmandu were also statistically significant. This finding is in line with previous findings, which showed that the programme appears to have had its greatest impact in areas outside the capital.

In terms of changes in women's lives, respondents in the reference group in Kathmandu as well as in other parts of Nepal indicated significantly greater positive changes than the users and beneficiaries. The users and beneficiaries of the programme in areas outside Kathmandu, in turn, indicated significantly bigger positive changes in women's lives than the users and beneficiaries in Kathmandu. Thus, even if the programme in a relative sense seems to have had a smaller impact on women's lives, the finding is consistent with the findings related to changes in the availability of jobs, the level of poverty, the environment, and human and social capital. These indicate that the programme appears to have had its biggest positive impact in areas outside the capital Kathmandu.

Appendix B

Details of the perceived value of the UNV programme and other findings of the study

Table B.1   Perceived value of the work and performance of the Volunteers ($n = 169$, figures indicate per cent)

Items	Assessment by the users and beneficiaries			
	Poor or very poor	OK	Good or very good	Total
Relevance of the work of the Volunteers	3.6	30.5	65.9	100.0
Effectiveness of the Volunteers	5.3	33.7	61.0	100.0
Performance of the Volunteers compared to other Volunteers	5.1	25.4	69.5	100.0
Performance of the Volunteers compared to international experts	8.9	37.9	53.2	100.0
Performance of the Volunteers compared to other non-nationals	4.3	25.9	69.8	100.0
Performance of the Volunteers compared to nationals of Nepal	4.9	42.0	53.1	100.0
Results of the work of the Volunteers	3.0	24.9	72.1	100.0
Continuation of activities started by the Volunteers	10.8	37.4	51.8	100.0
Long-term benefits of the work of the Volunteers	8.4	28.1	63.5	100.0

Table B.2   Assessment by the users and beneficiaries of different UNV-related factors and their possible effect on the work of the Volunteers ($n = 100$ or 169, figures indicate per cent)

| | Assessment by the users and beneficiaries | | | |
Items	Very poor or poor	OK	Good or very good	Total
Competence of Volunteers	1.2	23.8	75.0	100.0
Motivation of Volunteers	1.2	24.3	74.5	100.0
Matching with post	10.4	25.0	64.6	100.0
Recruitment process	6.6	33.0	60.4	100.0

| | Assessment by the users and beneficiaries | | | |
Items	Negative or very negative	None	Positive or very positive	Total
Briefing given to hosts	7.7	14.3	78.0	100.0
Language training	16.5	25.3	58.2	100.0
Other training	7.1	21.4	71.5	100.0
Living allowance	5.4	50.0	44.6	100.0
Length of assignment	41.2	22.7	36.1	100.0
Working for the UN	0.6	8.6	90.8	100.0
Working as a Volunteer	1.2	12.6	86.2	100.0
UN rules and procedures	17.3	77.4	5.3	100.0
UNV rules and procedures	11.4	84.3	4.3	100.0

Table B.3   Assessment by the Volunteers of different UNV-
related factors and their possible effect on their
work ($n = 48$, figures indicate per cent)

| | Assessment by the Volunteers | | | |
Items	Very poor or poor	OK	Good or very good	Total
Matching with post	4.2	16.7	79.2	100.0
Recruitment process	6.3	18.8	75.0	100.0

| | Assessment by the Volunteers | | | |
Items	Negative or very negative	None	Positive or very positive	Total
Briefing given to hosts	14.0	14.0	72.0	100.0
Language training	13.3	17.8	68.9	100.0
Other training	7.8	17.8	74.4	100.0
Length of assignment	16.7	33.3	50.0	100.0
Living allowance	20.5	54.5	25.0	100.0
Other entitlements	6.7	33.3	60.0	100.0
Conditions of service	6.7	30.3	63.0	100.0
Job description	4.2	20.8	75.0	100.0
Management/supervision	6.7	17.8	75.5	100.0
Co-worker availability	13.6	15.9	70.5	100.0
UN rules and procedures	4.4	68.9	26.7	100.0
UNV rules and procedures	4.4	63.7	31.9	100.0

Table B.4   Assessment by the users and beneficiaries of the effect of institutional factors on the work of the Volunteers ($n = 169$, figures indicate per cent)

| Items | Assessment by the users and beneficiaries | | | |
	Negative or very negative	None	Positive or very positive	Total
Link to other government agencies	5.1	6.6	88.2	100.0
Link to international organizations	3.2	15.9	80.9	100.0
Link to non-governmental organizations (NGOs)	3.0	10.4	86.6	100.0
Financial support from the government	7.3	68.3	24.4	100.0
Financial support from the UN	3.5	16.1	80.4	100.0
Financial support from international organizations	4.3	42.7	53.0	100.0
Other support from the government	4.5	41.0	54.5	100.0
Other support from the UN	2.3	29.7	68.0	100.0
Other support from international organizations	3.4	48.3	48.3	100.0
Rules and procedures of the government	13.9	84.1	2.0	100.0
Rules and procedures of NGOs	4.3	91.4	4.3	100.0

Table B.5   Assessment by the Volunteers of the effect of institutional factors on their work ($n = 48$, figures indicate per cent)

Items	Assessment by the Volunteers			
	Negative or very negative	None	Positive or very positive	Total
Link to other government agencies	6.5	2.2	91.3	100.0
Link to international organizations	5.0	7.5	87.5	100.0
Link to non-governmental organizations (NGOs)	6.8	9.1	84.1	100.0
Financial support from the government	18.8	31.2	50.0	100.0
Financial support from the UN	9.8	9.8	80.4	100.0
Financial support from international organizations	0.0	25.7	74.3	100.0
Other support from the government	9.3	18.6	72.1	100.0
Other support from the UN	7.7	2.6	89.7	100.0
Other support from international organizations	0.0	18.4	81.6	100.0
Rules and procedures of the government	20.5	70.4	9.1	100.0
Rules and procedures of NGOs	4.4	80.8	14.8	100.0

Table B.6   Assessment by the users of the effect of external factors on the work of the Volunteers ($n = 100$, figures indicate per cent)

| | Assessment by the users | | | |
| | Negative or | | Positive or | |
Items	very negative	None	very positive	Total
Climate	19.8	79.2	1.0	100.0
Social and cultural situation	9.3	88.7	2.0	100.0
Economic situation	18.3	73.1	8.6	100.0
Political situation	20.6	76.3	3.1	100.0
Security situation	9.1	89.9	1.0	100.0

Table B.7   Assessment by the Volunteers of the effect of external factors on their work ($n = 48$, figures indicate per cent)

| | Assessment by the Volunteers | | | |
| | Negative or | | Positive or | |
Items	very negative	None	very positive	Total
Climate	22.9	70.8	6.3	100.0
Social and cultural situation	20.0	64.5	15.5	100.0
Economic situation	34.9	55.8	9.3	100.0
Political situation	40.4	55.3	4.3	100.0
Security situation	10.4	83.3	6.3	100.0

Table B.8   Assessment by the Volunteers of the benefits of
their assignments to themselves (*n* = 48, figures
indicate per cent)

Items	Assessment by the Volunteers			
	None or very little	*Some*	*A lot or very much*	*Total*
Skills or knowledge learned	8.4	12.5	79.2	100.0
Cultural understanding	2.1	10.4	87.5	100.0
Influence on new job	34.8	32.6	32.6	100.0

Appendix C

List of evaluations and reviews of the UNV programme

Evaluations and reviews undertaken in 1996

Togo	Assistance Multisectorielle au Developpement Local
Burkina Faso	Appui Multisectoriel au Governement du Burkina Faso
Sierra Leone	Support to the Health Sector
Bhutan	Country Programme Review
	Human Resources Development
	Forest Resources Management and Institutional Development
	Strengthening Technical Manpower Capabilities
	Netherlands Facility for UNV Support from Central Europe
Botswana	Country Programme Review
	Teacher Training Programme
	Training for Primary Health Care
	Drought Relief Programme of Labour Intensive Works

Support to 1995 Global Women's Conference
Activities

Thematic   Design and Implementation of Special
                  Voluntary Fund Projects

                  UNV's Role as an Executing Agent

                  UNV's Experience with National Volunteers

                  UNV's Experience with Humanitarian
                  Assistance, Democratization and Peace-
                  building Activities

Evaluations and reviews undertaken in 1995

Benin   Renforcements des Capacités des Organisations
                  de Développement Comunitaire de Base

Chad   Assistance Multisectorielle au Gouvernement
                  Tchadien

Guinea Bissau   Assistance Spécial des Médicins Cubains

Lesotho   Grassroots Initiatives Support Project

Nigeria   UNV Assistance to the Health Sector

Tanzania   Multisectoral Assistance

Zambia   UNV Support to HIV/AIDS Prevention and
                  Care

                  Paramedical Training in Zambia

Costa Rica   Sustainable Human Development in Costa Rica

Kyrgystan   Evaluation of the United Nations Short-term
                  Advisory Services

Regional   Central American Human Rights Initiatives for
                  Grassroots Communities

                  Support to Local Initiatives in Latin America

Finland Fully Funded Posts

UNV's Decentralized Facilities to Support
Community-focused Work

Evaluations and reviews undertaken in 1994

Gambia	Gambia Development Village Trust Fund
Niger	Assistance à l'Enseignment Supérieur
	Assistance Multisectorielle
Global	UNV Programme Officer Scheme
Desk Reviews	Special Voluntary Fund Projects 1988–1993
	UNV Activities in the Health Sector

Evaluations and reviews undertaken in 1993

Cambodia	UNV Support to the UN Advance Mission in Cambodia
	Collaboration between the UN Transitional Authority in Cambodia and UNV
Mozambique	UNV Multisectoral Project
	Emergency Assistance to Central and Provincial Hospitals in Mozambique
Lesotho	Grassroots Initiatives Support Project
Uganda	Netherlands Support to UNV Domestic Development Service
Niger	Renforcement des Capacités de Développement Communautaire des Organisations de Base
Botswana	Primary Health Care Programme
Desk Reviews	UNV Activities in the Education Sector

Evaluations and reviews undertaken in 1992

China	UNV Assistance Project Phase II
	Establishment of the South-West China Secondary School English Training Centre
	Fully Funded Japanese Language Teachers
Papua New Guinea	Development of Provincial Sports and Recreation Programme
	UNV Multisectoral Project II
Namibia	Evaluation of Multisectoral Contingency Personnel for Namibia
Sudan	Kordofan Area Development Scheme
	North Darfour Area Development Schemes
	Planning Support for Darfour Development & Drought Management
Burkina Faso	Renforcement des Capacites d'Auto-Developpement Communautaire
Regional	Emergency Assistance to Drought Affected Countries in Sub-Saharan Africa
	UNV Assistance to Arab Least Developed Countries Phase II

Evaluations and reviews undertaken in 1991

Afghanistan	Country Programme Review
Yemen	Country Programme Review
Guyana	Country Programme Review
Botswana	Country Programme Review
	UNV Assistance to the Education Sector

	UNV Assistance to the Health Sector
	Multisectoral Support
Burkina Faso	Multisectoral (Appui Technique et Operationnel)
	Multisectoral (Encadrement Technique et Perfectionnement de Formateurs)
Central African Republic	Multisectoral Support
Comoros	Multisectoral Support
Samoa	UNVs for the Health Department
Zambia	UNV Support to Youth and Domestic Development Service
Thematic	UNV as a Channel for Micro-Capital Assistance

Evaluations and reviews undertaken in 1990

Niger	Appui à l'Universite de Niamey
	Multisectoral Support
Fiji	UNV Assistance to the Health Sector
Lesotho	UNVs in Community-based Development
	Development of Rural Technologies
	Mapotu Village Community Development
Regional	Review of UNDP-UNV/Domestic Development Service Programme in the Pacific Region

Evaluations and reviews undertaken in 1989

Sierra Leone	Country Programme Review
Samoa	Country Programme Review

Bangladesh	Assistance to Kumudini Hospital
Bhutan	Strengthening Technical Manpower Capabilities
Samoa	UNVs for Education Department
Central African Republic	Formation Acceleree d'Enseignants de Sciences et Technologie du Niveau Secondaire
Tanzania	Women's Appropriate Food Technology Project
Regional	Strengthening of National NGOs and Governmental Organizations for Community Level in the Africa Region
	Strengthening of Indigenous and Government Bodies Promoting Self-reliance at the Community-level in the Asia Region

Bibliography

Books and articles

Barro Robert J. and Xavier Sala-i-Martin. *Economic Growth*. New York: McGraw-Hill, 1995.

Becker, Gary S. *Human Capital: A Theoretical and Empirical Approach with Special Reference to Education*. New York: The Columbia University Press for NBER, 1964 (Chicago: The University of Chicago Press, 1993, reprint).

Blakie, Piers, John Cameron, and David Seddon. *Nepal in Crises: Growth and Stagnation at the Periphery*. Oxford: Clarendon Press, 1980.

Blaug, Mark. *The Methodology of Economics: or How Economists Explain*, 2nd edn. Cambridge, UK: Cambridge University Press, 1994.

Boruch, Robert F. and Werner Wothke, eds. *Randomization and Field Experimentation*. San Francisco: Jossey-Bass, 1985.

Carvalho, Soniya and Howard White. *Implementing Projects for the Poor: What Has Been Learned?* Directions in Development. Washington, DC: World Bank, 1996.

Cassen, Robert and Associates. *Does Aid Work?: Report to an Intergovernmental Task Force*, 2nd edn. New York: Oxford University Press, 1994.

Caudle, Sharon L. "Using Qualitative Approaches". In: *Handbook of Practical Program Evaluation*, eds. Joseph S. Wholey, Harry P. Hatry, and Kathryn E. Newcomer, San Francisco: Jossey-Bass, 1994, pp. 84–93.

Cernea, Michael, ed. *Putting People First: Sociological Variables in Rural Development*, 2nd edn. New York: Oxford University Press, 1991.

Childers, Erskine with Brian Urquhart. *Renewing the United Nations System*. Uppsala: Dag Hammarskjold Foundation, 1994.

Coleman, James S. *Foundations of Social Theory*. Cambridge, MA: Harvard University Press, 1990.

Commission on Global Governance. *Our Global Neighbourhood*. Oxford: Oxford University Press, 1995.

Cook, Thomas H. and Donald T. Campbell. *Quasi Experimentation: Design and Analysis Issues for Field Setting*. Boston: Houghton-Mifflin, 1979.

Dadzie, Kenneth. "The UN and the Problem of Economic Development". In: *United Nations, Divided World*, eds. Adam Roberts and Benedict Kingsbury, 2nd edn. New York: Oxford University Press, 1993, pp. 297–326.

Eberstadt, Nicholas. "The Impact of UN's 'Development Activities' on Third World Development". In: *Delusions of Grandeur. The United Nations and Global Intervention*, ed. Ted Galen Carpentier. Washington, DC: The Cato Institute, 1997, pp. 213–225.

Gillis Malcolm, Dwight H. Perkins, Michael Roemer, and Donald R. Snodgrass. *Economics of Development*, 3rd edn. New York: W. W. Norton & Co., 1992.

Goodrich, Leland M. "From League of Nations to United Nations". *International Organization* 1: 3–21, 1947.

Psacharopoulos, George and Maureen Woodhall. *Education for Development. An Analysis of Investment Choices*. Washington, DC: Oxford University Press for the World Bank, 1985.

Haq, Mahbub ul. *Reflections on Human Development*. New York: Oxford University Press, 1996.

International Labour Office. *Guidelines for the Preparation of Independent Evaluations of ILO Programmes and Projects*, Evaluation Unit, PROG/EVAL. Geneva: ILO, 1997.

Israel, Arturo. *Institutional Development: Incentives to Performance*. Baltimore: Johns Hopkins Press, 1987.

Jakobson, Max. *The United Nations in the 1990s. A Second Chance?* New York: Twentieth Century Books, 1993.

Jolly, Richard. "Human Development: The World After Copenhagen". *Global Governance: A Review of Multilateralism and International Organizations* 3 (May–August): 233–248, 1997.

Karan, Pradyumna P. and Hiroshi Ishii. *Nepal: A Himalayan Kingdom in Transition*. Tokyo: The United Nations University Press, 1996.

Kaufmann, Johann and Nico Schrijver. *Changing Global Needs: The Expanding Roles for the United Nations System*. Hanover, NH: The Academic Council on the United Nations System, 1990.

Kaufmann, Johann, Dick Leurdijk, and Nico Schrijver. *The World in Turmoil: Testing the UN's Capacity*. Hanover, NH: The Academic Council on the United Nations System, 1991.

Kirgis, Frederic L. Jr. *International Organizations in their Legal Setting*, 2nd edn. St. Paul: West Publishing Co., 1993.

Krippendorff, Klaus. *Content Analysis: An Introduction to Its Methodology*. Thousand Oaks, CA: Sage, 1980.

Krugman, Paul. "The Myth of the Asian Miracle". *Foreign Affairs* 73 (November–December): 62–78, 1994.

MacArthur, John D. "Logical Frameworks Today – Increased Diversification of the Planning Format". In: *Cost-benefit Analysis and Project Appraisal in Developing Countries*, eds. Colin Kirkpatrick and Jon Weiss. Brookfield, VT: Edward Elgar, 1996, pp. 128–143.

Marsden, David and Peter Oakley, eds. *Evaluating Social Development Projects*, Development Guidelines 5. Oxford: Oxfam, 1990.

Nordic UN Project. *The United Nations in Development. Reform Issues in the Economic and Social Fields. A Nordic Perspective*. Stockholm: Almqvist & Wiksell, 1991.

Organisation for Economic Co-operation and Development. *Principles for Evaluation of Development Assistance*, Development Assistance Committee, OCDE/GD 208. Paris: OECD, 1991.

Organisation for Economic Co-operation and Development. *Development Cooperation Report, 1995*, Development Assistance Committee. Paris: OECD, 1996.

Organisation for Economic Co-operation and Development. *Development Cooperation Report, 1998*, Development Assistance Committee. Paris: OECD, 1999.

Psacharopoulos, George and Maureen Woodhall. *Education for Development. An Analysis of Investment Choices*. Washington, DC: Oxford University Press for the World Bank, 1985, pp. 46–53.

Putnam, Robert. *Making Democracy Work: Civic Traditions in Modern Italy*. Princeton, NJ: Princeton University Press, 1993.

Report of the Independent Working Group on the Future of the United Nations. *The United Nations in its Second Half-Century*. New Haven, CT: Yale University Printing Service, 1995.

Riddell, Roger C., Stein-Erik Kruse, Timo Kyllonen, Satu Ojanpera, and Jean-Louis Vielajus. *Searching for Impact and Methods: NGO Evaluation Synthesis Study*, Ministry for Foreign Affairs of Finland, Department for International Development Cooperation, Report 1997:2. Helsinki: Hakapaino, 1998.

Roberts, Adam and Benedict Kingsbury. "The UN's Roles in International Society since 1945". In: *United Nations, Divided World*, eds. Adam Roberts and Benedict Kingsbury, 2nd edn. New York: Oxford University Press, 1993, pp. 1–62.

Sarel, Michael. "Growth and Productivity in ASEAN Economies", paper presented at a conference of the International Monetary Fund in Jakarta, Indonesia, November 1996.

Strategic Planning Associates and C.A.C. International. "Effects of Canadian Volunteer Sending". Ottawa, 1994.

Union Bank of Switzerland. "The Asian Economic Miracle". *UBS International Finance* 29 (Autumn), 1996.

United Nations Administrative Committee on Coordination. *Monitoring and Evaluation: Guiding Principles*. Rome: IFAD Publications, 1985.

United Nations Children's Fund. *Making a Difference: A UNICEF Guide to Monitoring and Evaluation*. New York: UNICEF, 1991.

United Nations Development Programme. *How to Write a Project Document*. New York: UNDP, 1990.

United Nations Development Programme. *Human Development Report*. New York: Oxford University Press, 1992.

United Nations Development Programme. *Human Development Report*. New York: Oxford University Press, 1996.

United Nations Development Programme. *Human Development Report*. New York: Oxford University Press, 1997.

United Nations Development Programme. *Results-oriented Monitoring and Evaluation*, Office of Evaluation and Strategic Planning, UNDP/OESP. New York: UNDP, 1997.

United Nations Volunteers. *Volunteers against Conflict*. Tokyo: United Nations University Press, 1996.

United Nations Volunteers. "The Appropriate Use of Volunteers in Development". *United Nations Volunteers Thematic Series*, Programme Advisory Note. Geneva: UNV, 1991.

United Nations Volunteers. *UNV at a Glance – The Key Statistics*. Geneva: UNV, 1990–1996.

United Nations Volunteers. *Strategy 2000: Strategic Approach 1997– 2000*. Bonn: UNV, 1997.

United Nations Volunteers. *UNV at a Glance – The Key Statistics*. Bonn: UNV, 1997–1998.

Valadez, Joseph and Michael Bamberger, eds. *Monitoring and Evaluating Social Programs in Developing Countries*, EDI Development Studies. Washington, DC: The World Bank, 1994.

Wilson, Irene and Marjon Nooter, eds. *Evaluation of Finnish Personnel as Volunteers in Development Cooperation*, Ministry of Foreign Affairs in Finland, Department for International Development Cooperation, Report 1995:3. Helsinki: Hakapaino, 1995.

World Bank. *The East Asian Miracle: Economic Growth and Public Policy*. New York: Oxford University Press, 1993.

World Bank. "Evaluating Development Operations: Methods for

Judging Outcomes and Impacts". *Lessons & Practices*, Operations Evaluation Department, Number 10 (July). Washington, DC: World Bank, 1997.

World Bank. *World Development Report*. Washington, DC: Oxford University Press for the World Bank, 1997.

World Institute for Development Economics Research of the United Nations University. *World Economic Summits: The Role of Representative Groups in the Governance of the World Economy*, Study Group Series No. 4. Helsinki: WIDER, 1989.

United Nations documents

Charter of the United Nations.

Economic and Social Council Resolution 849 (XXXII). "Use of Volunteer Workers in the Operational Programmes of the United Nations and Related Agencies Designed to Assist in the Economic and Social Development of the Less Developed Countries". 3 August 1961.

Economic and Social Council Resolution 1444 (XLVII). "Utilization of Volunteers in United Nations Development Projects". 7 August 1969.

General Assembly Resolution 1710 (XVI). "United Nations Development Decade". 18 December 1961.

General Assembly Resolution 2460 (XXIII). "Human Resources for Development". 20 December 1968.

General Assembly Resolution 2542 (XXIV). "Declaration on Social Progress and Development". 11 December 1969.

General Assembly Resolution 2626 (XXIV). "International Development Strategy for the Second United Nations Development Decade". 24 October 1970.

General Assembly Resolution 2688 (XXV). "The Capacity of the United Nations Development System". 11 December 1970.

General Assembly Resolution 2659 (XXV). "United Nations Volunteers". 17 December 1970.

General Assembly Resolution 3201 (S-VI). "A New International Economic Order". 1 May 1974.

General Assembly Resolution 31/131. "United Nations Volunteers Programme". 7 February 1977.

General Assembly Resolution 31/166. "United Nations Volunteers". 14 February 1977.

General Assembly Resolution 35/56. "International Development Strategy for the Third United Nations Development Decade". 5 December 1980.

General Assembly Resolution 40/212. "International Volunteers Day". 17 December 1985.

General Assembly Resolution 41/128. "Declaration on the Right to Development". 4 December 1986.

General Assembly Resolution 44/211. "Triennial Policy Review of Operational Activities for Development of the United Nations System". 23 February 1990.

General Assembly Resolution S-18/3. "Declaration on International Economic Cooperation, in Particular the Revitalization of Economic Growth and Development of the Developing Countries". 1 May 1990.

General Assembly Resolution 45/177. "Restructuring and Revitalization of the United Nations in the Economic, Social and Related Fields". 19 December 1990.

General Assembly Resolution 45/199. "International Development Strategy for the Fourth United Nations Development Decade". 21 December 1990.

General Assembly Resolution 45/264. "Restructuring and Revitalization of the United Nations in the Economic, Social and Related Fields". 13 May 1991.

General Assembly Resolution 46/235. "Restructuring and Revitalization of the United Nations in the Economic, Social and Related Fields". 13 April 1992.

General Assembly Resolution 47/199. "Triennial Policy Review of Operational Activities for Development of the United Nations System". 22 December 1992.

General Assembly Resolution 48/162. "Further Measures for the Restructuring and Revitalization of the United Nations in the Economic, Social and Related Fields". 14 January 1994.

General Assembly Resolution 50/120. "Triennial Policy Review of Operational Activities for Development of the United Nations System". 16 February 1996.

General Assembly Resolution 50/227. "Further Measures for the Restructuring and Revitalization of the United Nations in the Economic, Social and Related Fields". 16 May 1996.

General Assembly Resolution 51/240. "Agenda for Development". 20 June 1997.

General Assembly Resolution 52/17. "International Year of Volunteers, 2001". 20 November 1997.

General Assembly Resolutions 53/192. "Triennial Policy Review of Operational Activities for Development of the United Nations System". 25 February 1999.

United Nations Development Programme Governing Council decision 87/16. "Human Resources Development". 18 June 1987.

United Nations Development Programme Governing Council decision 87/36. "United Nations Volunteers". 19 June 1987.

United Nations Development Programme Governing Council decision 88/29. "Experience in Human Resources Development". 1 July 1988.

United Nations Development Programme Governing Council decision 89/20. "The Role of the United Nations Development Programme in the 1990s". 30 June 1989.

United Nations Development Programme Governing Council decision 90/34. "Fifth Programming Cycle". 23 June 1990.

United Nations Development Programme Executive Board decision 94/14. "UNDP: Initiative for Change". 10 June 1994.

Report of the Preparatory Commission of the United Nations, PC/20. 23 December 1945.

Note by the Secretary-General to the Economic and Social Council E/4663. "Utilization of Volunteers in United Nations Development Projects". 16 May 1969.

Report by the Secretary-General to the General Assembly A/50/202/Add.1. "Comprehensive Statistical Data on Operational Activities for Development for the Year 1994". 25 September 1995.

Report by the Secretary-General to the Economic and Social Council E/1997/65. "Progress in the Implementation of General Assembly Resolution 50/120". 11 June 1997.

Report by the Secretary-General to the General Assembly A/51/950. "Renewing the United Nations: A Programme for Reform". 16 July 1997.

Report by the Secretary-General to the General Assembly A/53/226. "Triennial Policy Review of Operational Activities for Development of the United Nations System". 12 August 1998.

Report of the Executive Board of the United Nations Development Programme, DP/1996/19, Annual Session, Geneva, 6–17 May 1996. 23 May 1996.

Report of the Administrator to the Governing Council of the United Nations Development Programme DP/1988/62. "Experience in Human Resource Development Since 1970". 15 March 1988.

Report of the Administrator to the Governing Council of the United Nations Development Programme DP/1988/46/Add.1. "Review of the United Nations Volunteers". 23 March 1988.

Report of the Administrator to the Executive Board of the United Nations Development Programme DP/1997/30/Add.1. "Information on United Nations System Regular and Extrabudgetary Technical Cooperation Expenditures Financed from Sources other than UNDP". 16 July 1997.

Report by the United Nations Joint Inspection Unit JIU/REP/95/2. "Accountability, Management Improvement, and Oversight in the United Nations System". 1995.

Index

analysis of variance (ANOVA)
109, 120
assessments *see* impact evaluations
assignments
costs of 23, 28
length of 77–78
see also volunteers
attitudes, changes in 113–114
see also social capital

Becker, Gary S. 31, 85
Bretton Woods Institutions *see*
International Monetary
Fund; World Bank

Canadian volunteer sending
programmes 39
community workers 22
comprehensive triennial policy
reviews 14
conceptual framework 50–53, 54
conferences 9
conference fatigue 11
global conferences 11–12
follow-up 11–12
control groups 101, 102
cooperation, changes in 114–116
see also social capital
Costa Rica 49
costs of volunteer assignments 23,
28
counterfactual situation 39, 47,
102

data collection/analysis 53–63
objectivity 63
relevance 63

reliability 59–62
validity 57–59
declarations 9
development cooperation
effectiveness of 1–2
impact of 30
volunteer work 17
see also economic development
documentation
need for improvement 100–102
poor quality of records 89–90,
100–102
reports of volunteers 45–46, 90

Earth Summit 11
Economic and Social Council
(ECOSOC) 7–10, 15, 27
economic development 24
education and 31
UN commitment to 7–10
see also development cooperation
Economic Security Council 10
education, economic growth and
31
see also training
environmental protection 15,
33–34
UNV programme impact
assessment 72–73, 85,
86–87, 124–125, 128,
129
exchange programmes 94–95
Executive Committee for
Development 10
Expanded Programme for
Technical Assistance
12–13